# SEEKING A NEW WORLD

# SEEKING A NEW WORLD

A New Philosophy of Confucius
and Kim Hang

**Sung Jang Chung**

iUniverse, Inc.
New York   Bloomington

# Seeking a New World
## A New Philosophy of Confucius and Kim Hang

iUniverse books may be ordered through booksellers or by contacting:

iUniverse
1663 Liberty Drive
Bloomington, IN 47403
www.iuniverse.com
1-800-Authors (1-800-288-4677)

Because of the dynamic nature of the Internet, any Web addresses or links contained in this book may have changed since publication and may no longer be valid. The views expressed in this work are solely those of the author and do not necessarily reflect the views of the publisher, and the publisher hereby disclaims any responsibility for them.

ISBN: 978-1-4401-8601-1 (pbk)
ISBN: 978-1-4401-8599-1 (cloth)
ISBN: 978-1-4401-8600-4 (ebook)

Printed in the United States of America

iUniverse rev. date: 11/18/09

# CONTENTS

# ILLUSTRATIONS

# ACKNOWLEDGMENTS

I humbly express my deepest gratitude to Gautama Buddha, Maitreya Buddha, Jesus, Confucius, Kim Hang, and Paramahansa Yogananda for their supernal teachings that have been showing me the path of self-realization. I would like to acknowledge those authors cited in the references section of this book for their intellectual help, support, and validation of my work, as well as those authors not cited there for their knowledge contributing to the development of the theories written in this book.

I am very thankful to Dr. Chong Chul Yook for his lifelong encouragement in our study of the *Jeong Yeok*, and his valuable review of my manuscript related to the *Jeong Yeok*. I would like to specially express my sincere gratitude to the late Dr. Jeong Ho Yi for his teachings in his outstanding books on the subjects of the *Jeong Yeok* and the *I Ching*, which he sent me personally after their publications in Korea, and decades-long encouragement in my study of the *Jeong Yeok* and the *I Ching*. I am also thankful to the late Kyung Un Kim for his personal lectures on the *Jeong Yeok* and the *I Ching* that I received at a young age in Korea.

I am grateful to Dr. C. W. Sheppard for his teaching and encouragement in my study of computer programming at the University of Tennessee Graduate School. Without his help, my research in searching for a general mathematical model of the "probacent"-probability equation applicable in biomedical phenomena would not have been successfully accomplished. In this regard, I would like to express my deep gratitude to Chung Chin Kim, PhD, for his valuable contributions and outstanding achievements in our biomedical research at the Catholic Medical College in Seoul, Korea.

I am pleased to acknowledge the publishers' granting of permissions to quote or copy figures of their authors' books, and I am particularly grateful to Sarah McKechnie, president of the Lucis Trust, and Eunjin Kim, president of Asian Culture Press in Seoul, Korea.

I would like to specially express my deep and sincere thanks to my wife, Kwang Jun Lee, MD, for her more than five decades of help in my work in our up-and-down life together, and her unsurpassed patience and love.

# INTRODUCTION

In my middle-school days in Korea, my father got a comprehensive collection of Buddhist scripture for me to read. I read sermons of Gautama Buddha and was fascinated by the Buddha's *Dhammapada* as written in chapter 2 of this book. I started to imagine an unseen religious world, and I longed to see for myself the true invisible world.

At the same period of my childhood, together with my parents, I experienced the existence of a mysterious spiritual world through a medium that acted as a channel to the Other Side. I was almost convinced about the coexistence of an invisible and inconceivable spiritual world. I came to be interested in exploring the spiritual world of religion. I decided to study religion and metaphysics as well as science of the physical world (chapters 1 and 2).

I was imprisoned by Japanese colonial police for my participation in an underground organization of Korea's independence movement when I was a medical student in Korea during World War II in 1944 and 1945. In a prison cell, I dreamed an unexpected precognitive dream, foretelling the exact date of my release from prison. I believe that the special dream was a revelation from heaven (chapter 2).

During the Korean War (1950–3), I also dreamed an extraordinary precognitive dream in North Korea, where I had been forcefully taken by invading North Korean communist agents. I received a vision in the dream that revealed a specific date, a natural landscape, and an event that would take place in near future. The dream came true in reality, saving not only me but also scores of other people (chapter 3).

When I was young, I went to Mount Kyeryong in Korea to study the *Jeong Yeok* (正易), a Korean philosophy book written by Kim Hang (金恒), and to do meditation. Fortunately, I was able to have blissful opportunities to listen to sermons of Jesus, Confucius, Kim Hang, and Po'eon Chung (鄭圃隱), my nineteenth ancestor, especially voices of God through an extraordinary medium, Jeong Kwan Song (chapter 11). Tears were flowing on my cheeks, and my heart was pounding with awe and joy beyond description when I humbly and respectfully listened to the voices spoken by the medium.

From my teenage years to this day, I have so eagerly longed to find out the truth about the universe and life—the ultimate truth of religion and science. I believe that science and religion are one; the truth would unify science and religion without conflict (chapters 5, 6, and 7).

I have been, however, trying to avoid misunderstanding, dogmatism, and false conceptions. I was astounded and impressed by the new quantum theories proposed by Dr. David Bohm, the great physicist, which I describe in chapter 8.

In modern science, many important scientific findings have been discovered in the physical world and the realm of consciousness and seem to be supportive of Bohm's quantum theories (chapter 9). I describe coexisting physical and spiritual worlds in chapter 10. In Part VI, I write about the book of *Jeong Yeok* (正易), translated as *Right Changes*) written by Kim Hang (金恒) in 1885, that describes the coming of a new world and the age of Maitreya Buddha.

This book includes my personal metaphysical experiences that are undeniable facts to me (chapter 11). This book expresses my personal opinions and beliefs; therefore, readers may have different interpretations.

This book is written with my sincere intention to serve brothers and sisters who seek truth in life, and to serve God.

# PART ONE

## Unforgettable Experiences in My Life

# — CHAPTER 1 —

## The Story of My Pleurisy Treatment and Carp

I was admitted to Kyungbuk Middle School in Taegu City after my graduation from Pohang Elementary School in Pohang, Korea. I left my parents for the first time to study for a higher education. At Pohang Railway Station, I boarded a train that was much smaller than an old amusement-park train. I got to Taegu City after two or three hours. If I had taken a current, modern train, surely it would have taken less than one hour.

I stayed at a boarding house. I was fond of study and happy to have a higher education in a new school and a larger city. Although I thought of my parents at my hometown, I diligently attended the middle school.

I got my school report card at the end of the first year (the seventh grade). I came from a small town but came first place in my entire class, ahead of many boys from Taegu City. The next day, spring vacation started. I was so happy to go home to see my parents. I went to school early in the morning and ran in the empty school playground for joy. That afternoon, I got back to my home on the first vacation in my life. My parents were so happy to see me. I showed them my report card,

3

showing I had won first place. They were very pleased to see it and proud of their son.

One day that spring when I advanced to the second year (the eighth grade), I suddenly developed a high fever, headache, shortness of breath, and malaise. I was lying in the boarding house room away from school. I felt vague and confused.

That evening, my cousin who was a student of Kaesung High School in Taegu City happened to visit me and found me so sick with fever. He called a doctor from Choongang Hospital for a patient home visit.

The doctor came to my boarding house and examined me. He made a diagnosis of pleurisy with fluid in the chest. He aspirated a few cubic centimeters of pleural fluid with a syringe.

The memory of that night is unforgettable. My cousin told the doctor that my father was a medical doctor practicing in my hometown. After the doctor left, my cousin placed a long-distance call to my father, informing him of my severe illness of pleurisy with fluid in the chest.

My father told him, "I already knew that Sung Jang is suffering pleurisy with fluid in the chest. Bring him immediately to Pohang by taxi."

My cousin called a taxi and transported me to my hometown. I remember only getting into the taxi and riding in the dark night, half conscious and half sleeping. After two or three hours, I got home around midnight.

As soon as I reached the foyer of my house, I suddenly felt better. My consciousness felt almost clear, and later my pain and discomfort completely subsided.

I recall an old lady who was a close friend of my parents and often visited our home in my middle-school and high-school days. She was a medium who could communicate with a spirit. I understood a spirit as a personality without a physical body.

The old lady had visited my parents that day when my parents later got a long-distance call from my cousin. She told my parents, "Sung Jang in Taegu is suffering an illness with fluid in his chest."

My parents were shocked to hear the message from the spirit through the old lady medium. They got worried. She left our home after giving her message. Soon after she left, the long-distance call reached my parents. I later heard this story from my parents.

My father confirmed the diagnosis of exudative pleurisy by physical examination. He decided to have me withdraw from school temporarily and to treat me himself at home.

The next day, my father examined me and aspirated about one liter of straw-colored pleural fluid with a special large syringe. I took daily medical treatment with oral drugs and intravenous medication and absolute bed rest.

The teacher of my middle school class was notified of my temporary absence from school for a year due to my illness, which required medical treatment and rest at home. I continued to have a quiet inpatient's life at my father's hospital.

A few days passed, and my father found in his examination of me that the chest fluid had accumulated again like before. He told us his finding. Our family discussed it and wished that it would be better to treat my pleurisy with medication alone, instead of repeat aspiration with a large, thick needle. My parent felt that a repeat aspiration would be a painful procedure for me.

My mother asked the spirit a question when the lady visited us that day. "Sung Jang has a large amount of accumulated fluid in his chest again. What can we do? We wish to continue the current treatment without any more aspiration, if possible."

As soon as my mother's question ended, the spirit spoke through the medium's lips and answered. The old lady medium spoke with a low, whisper-like voice that was not clear and understandable to us. It seemed to me that the spirit was borrowing the medium's lips to communicate with us who were living in this world. Her eyes were half open. We were sitting quietly in the room. The medium appeared not to be in a state of trance; she seemed perfectly conscious when she spoke for the spirit. She understood the message from the spirit and conveyed it to us right away after the spirit finished speaking through her.

She said, "If you feel it is pitiful to do a repeat aspiration of the chest fluid, leave him without it and wait. Do not worry."

My farther listened to the spirit's answer and made up his mind not to perform a repeat aspiration of the chest fluid but instead to wait and observe me.

The next day my father re-examined me by auscultation and percussion. He was astonished to find that the re-accumulated chest fluid was completely gone! He told this unusual and amazing finding to us. There was no need of a repeat aspiration. Consequently, I did not undergo another thoracentesis until my complete recovery from pleurisy. I continued to receive daily my father's medical treatment with nutritional diet therapy and bed rest.

* * *

There is a special and really interesting story related to carp from when I was sick with pleurisy in my childhood. The spring of that year was over, and summer came. My father's sister's family lived in a village called Yunil, about five miles away from my hometown. Her husband went fishing to the nearby Hyungsan River when he had free time. The weather was hot in the daytime. If he could catch even a few carp, he would walk to our house with them. He gave them to us in order to help my nutritional diet therapy. Our servant cooked carp soup for me, and my mother gave it to me. Carp soup in summer was a valuable nutritional diet for patients.

We had a severe drought that summer. One early morning the old lady visited our home and said, "I have come here early this morning because the spirit asked me to come to Sung Jang's home and to give you some information." She continued, speaking for the spirit, "The water gate of the lake behind the mountains west of the City of Pohang was opened this morning to drain lake water in order to supply water to dry rice fields and farmland in drought. Crowds of people have gathered there. There are lots of carp in the water flowing out. Go quickly, and catch them for a nutritional supplement for Sung Jang."

My parents sent our two employees to the lake. They encountered the exact scene that the spirit had described. About two hours later, they came home with buckets full of many carp that they had caught at the lake.

My whole family was greatly surprised to see them in reality. Scores of carp were placed in the small pond (about twelve feet square) in our courtyard.

They planned to keep the carp alive in the pond, to be used for the purpose of my nutritional diet therapy. The scores of carp were vigorously swimming and moving around in the pond.

The next morning, my family went to see how the carp were doing in the pond. Unexpectedly, almost all of the carp were upside down, showing their bellies, and motionless. Such changes in their posture and behavior might indicate that the carp suffered severe stress from being caught by human hands, transportation from the lake to our house, and the new environment of our pond. The carp might have carried disease from the lake and developed the above-described signs on that day for the first time. If the skin of carp was damaged, the skin lesions might easily develop bacterial infection; when severe, it might become fatal (George C. Blasiora, *Koi* [10]).

My whole family was concerned and worried about the possible death of all the carp. The old lady visited our home that day. My mother told this fact to the spirit in our session. The medium was sitting in front of us; the spirit was invisible to us. I guessed that the spirit was not physical, but it seemed to be a personality existing beside the medium in the room. Our communication with the spirit was exclusively through the medium.

The spirit replied, through the medium, "Do not worry about the carp. Just keep them in the pond and use them for a nutritional diet food."

My family listened to the answer and decided to continue keeping the carp in the pond.

The next morning, my worried family went to the pond in order to see how the carp were doing. A wonderful phenomenon had occurred. None of the carp were found dead! The scores of carp were lively, moving around in the pond. This might suggest that the carp were able to adapt to the changes in the environment and recover overnight. It seems to me that the spirit might have foreseen the outcome of the carp with precognition or actually helped the carp adapt and recover. Either way it was inconceivable but helpful to our family in that situation.

From then on, I was able to eat carp soup for more than one month. We were overwhelmed with wonder, and it was thanks to the extraordinary recovery and survival of all of the carp.

I believed in heaven's grace through the spirit's help. I had no doubt of the existence of a mysterious unseen world.

My pleurisy was cured by my father's treatment and my mother's loving care as well as our family's employees and relatives' kind assistance for about three months, together with the extraordinary, unforgettable help of the spirit through the medium.

After a one-year absence from school, I returned to Taegu City. I restarted eighth grade, making new friends in the class. I could continue my study at middle school and high school.

In my Kyungbuk Middle School and High School days, I went to my parents' home in my hometown, Pohang, on school vacations. I heard the spirit speaking through the medium whenever she visited my parents. I would like to describe several issues from our sessions that I recall.

- According to the spirit's answer to our question about travel, the spirit could instantaneously go anywhere in Korea, Japan, or anyplace else if the spirit wished to go. The distance or the sea between Pohang and the destination had nothing to do with it. If I went to Seoul or Japan to study, the spirit could go and see me anytime without trouble. This is impossible with humans. It is a fascinating unseen world. It seems to me that the dimensions of the spiritual world are quite different from those of our physical world.

- Any human being who is born to this world, grows up, and does his or her proper profession that fits will be healthy physically. I, Sung Jang, was born to be a doctor. If I had a doctor's job, I will be healthy; otherwise I would not be healthy. I would be better off going to a medical school. The spirit advised us that the doctor's profession was divinely assigned work that would fit me in this life. This was the spirit's answer to our family's question of which school I should choose when I was applying for admission to colleges three years after my recovery from pleurisy.

- Through my inexplicable psychic experience in my childhood in which the spirit guided us as I described, I came to firmly believe that the visible physical world and the invisible, unknown spiritual world beyond the five senses mysteriously coexist in this universe. The memories I have shared with you have lived in my mind vividly since my childhood.

My family followed the advice of the spirit regarding my career. I took an entrance exam after high school and was accepted to the preparatory school of the Kyeongsung Imperial University College of Medicine (now the Seoul National University College of Medicine ) in Seoul, Korea.

The City of Pohang, where I was born as the second son to my parents in 1923, was a small fishing port in South Korea. Eighty years later, the city has developed and become a world-class industrial city where the Pohang Iron & Steel Company (POSCO) is located.

## — Chapter 2 —

# A Grandpa's Letter, for His Grandchildren

I received an unexpected long-distance call and a subsequent letter from one of my medical school classmates, Chong Suhl Kim, MD, in Seoul, Korea, in October 2005. I wrote a reply to him, describing a special event that had happened in our medical school days. He particularly asked me to write about it in detail. My wife and I felt that the event recorded in the letter was special and might be educational to our grandchildren in the future when they grew up and read it. So we gave a copy of my long letter to our eldest grandson in elementary school, who might grow up to be a medical doctor, telling him to read it when he grew up. I would like to present the letter in this book too.

Dear Chong Suhl,

I was greatly pleased to receive your unexpected long-distance call from my motherland, Korea, on October 18, 2005. I was overwhelmed with joy. I felt deep nostalgia. It is really a long time since we met last in Korea before I left for the United States.

I was also amazed to hear that the interrogation record of our case of the Hyeopdong Party independence movement prepared by the Japanese police was discovered by Kwang Se Lim, one of our medical school classmates, in the editorial room of the Korean national archives.

Ten days later, on October 28, I got your letter, accompanied by a copy of the interrogation record and your questionnaire. I appreciate your nice letter and the other documents you sent.

While I have been reading the interrogation record with great interest, I have been trying to recollect my experiences from six decades ago. As sixty years have passed since the liberation of Korea from Japanese colonial rule on August 15, 1945, this special news from you has made me think again that our lives are truly unpredictable. As a matter of fact, early this year, deep in my mind but half doubting it, I felt that an unusual event might happen this year, 2005, the year of Eulyu—same as the year 1945, the year of Eulyu in the sixty-year cycle of the lunar calendar, when the liberation of Korea took place.

I would like to answer your questionnaire and to write about some of my experiences from my young student life and to describe my feelings after reexamining the ideology of the Hyeopdong Party as well as my current beliefs and wishes.

## Imprisonment, Life behind Bars, and Experiences during the Period from My Release from Prison to Korean Liberation on August 15, 1945

### The Kyeonggi Province Police Station

In December 1944, when I was a sophomore medical student, I got up early one morning and was studying at my boarding house at Yeongeon-Dong, Seoul, in order to prepare for the year-end examination. All of a sudden, a group of Japanese police agents raided my boarding house and arrested me without any warrant. I was taken to the jail of the Security Section of the Kyeonggi Province Police Station.

It was a cold winter morning. I was sure that the kind Korean landlord of my boarding house must have been shocked by the unexpected raid by Japanese police. I have felt very sorry throughout my life that the landlord had to go through that yet unexplained, worrisome incident.

The Security Section of the Kyeonggi Province Police Station seemed to Koreans to be the headquarters of the Japanese police force in Korea that investigated and suppressed our Korean anti-Japanese independence movement patriots and underground organizations.

Interrogations by Japanese police took place every day. I became a subject of interrogation on an accused offense against the security law of Japanese colonial rule.

It is unknown to me even now how our case of the Hyeopdong Party was detected by Japanese police. At the time of my interrogation, it appeared to me that many facts of our underground independence movement that I knew had been found out and already were known to the interrogating police.

Torture was repeated every day unless the accused suspects admitted to incriminating acts or agreed with what the police wanted to hear.

The police agents beat us with clubs and kicked us with their shoes. A more severe torture was a water-suffocating torture that was indescribably barbaric and inhumane.

I was taken to a torture room early one morning. A cruel and atrocious-looking Japanese policeman and some other police agents tightly bound my entire body on a wooden plank and covered my face with a piece of cloth. Then they started pouring water on my cloth-covered face. I could not move or breathe. My mind became unclear and vague, and I lost consciousness during the asphyxiating, cruel torture. I do not know how long this torture lasted. All I recall is that at some later time, I was dragged by several police agents to the jail cell, and that I was left exhausted, supine, and stretched out on the cell floor. When I came to a little, I found myself surrounded by Korean detainees in the same cell, who were watching me with apparent worry and encouragement. This torture that I experienced is hardly forgettable, even now.

I guess that such brutal torture by Japanese police most likely killed many detained Korean patriots who fought for the anti-Japanese independence movement. I had already committed myself to doing as many good things as possible for our suppressed Korean people, and, if needed, to sacrificing my body. I had been inspired by the ideology of the Hyeopdong Party. My firm belief sustained me in jail.

I spent time ceaselessly in prayer and practiced *yeombul* ten thousand times: "*Nammu Amita-bul* (Amitabha), *Kwanseum-Bosal* (Avalokitesvara)." Prayer and *yeombul* allowed peace of mind, joy, and hope to arise within me. I did not regret my past actions, which I had done according to my youthful conscience and for righteousness. I had strong faith in a bright future for our country. My faith and beliefs helped me endure the physical and emotional abuse and difficulties behind bars I experienced until my release from prison.

To my surprise, there was a tiny hole in the wall between my cell and the neighboring cell. It was possible to secretly communicate with a low voice. One day, my name was called through the hole. I could not guess how in the world anyone in the neighboring cell knew of my presence in this cell.

The person who called my name in the secret communication was the late Sung Soo Lee, one of my medical school classmates. He asked me to inform the interrogating Japanese police of what he was going to tell me. He said, "I have nothing to do with your party, but I have been arrested and am here in the jail." He also asked me, "Would you please tell to the interrogating police agent that I have nothing to do with the party? Plead with him to release me."

I agreed to his request. The next morning, at the time of interrogation, I testified that Sung Soo Lee had nothing to do with the Hyeopdong Party. From the next day onward, the secret communications from Lee stopped. I assumed that he had been released, and this pleased me. Lee had a strong desire for learning and was one of my close classmates who was expected to become a great scholar in the future.

## Life behind Bars in the Seodemun Prison

One day in January 1945, as the police interrogations at the Kyeonggi Province Police Station seemed to have ended, I was transferred to the Seoul Seodemun Prison. That winter of 1945 was very cold. I was put in a relatively large cell where approximately twenty Korean detainees had already been placed in markedly crowded conditions.

The high windows of the cell were practically all broken. The prison cell was just like an outdoor field in the wild. Harshly cold wind blew directly into the room. The room temperature was probably around -10° C (14° F). It was freezing cold.

The concrete ceiling and the four surrounding walls were covered with ice. The ice began to freeze in early evening and continued to freeze during the night. After sunrise, the frozen ice started melting and falling down onto the floor, and onto our heads too.

The clothes that I wore were thin, blue, pajama-like prison apparel. I witnessed old people in the cell suffering frostbitten fingers and toes.

In the winter of 1944, there was a typhus epidemic caused by *Rickettsia provazekii* transmitted by human body lice, *Pediculus humanus corporis*. The principal clinical features are intense headache, chills, continuous fever, skin rash, and malaise. In untreated cases, some weak patients may develop azotemia from renal failure, agitation, stupor, coma, and death in the second week of the illness. Untreated epidemic typhus is fatal in 7–40 percent of cases, depending on the patient [13].

It is said that during certain outbreaks of typhus there was a 60 percent fatality rate among those infected; however, those patients who could survive became immune. Convalescence in those survivors was prolonged.

Luckily, broad-spectrum antibiotics such as chloramphenicol and tetracycline are now available and are highly efficient therapeutic agents against typhus. But during World War II, these antibiotics were, of course, unavailable.

Typhus prevailed in Seodemun Prison in that winter, 1944, infecting many prisoners and even prison guards watching prisoners in the cells. I heard that quite a number of patients died of typhus in the prison that winter.

Typhus developed in five or six patients (diagnosed based on clinical manifestations), one by one, in my prison cell. They were all transferred to the isolation ward of the prison as soon as they were discovered. There was no way to know the outcomes after their transfer.

I used to take care of those patients suspected of having typhus, keeping the patients beside me. Before long I suddenly developed quite similar signs and symptoms of headache, chills, and high fever. The prison guard was notified of my condition. I was immediately taken out of the cell and transferred to the isolation ward.

I was placed in a small isolation cell where another patient was lying on the floor and groaning. He was confused and had a high fever. There were two worn-out woven straw mats on the floor. Our daily rations consisted of only three lumps of miscellaneous mixed cereals, a bowl of salt water containing a few outer leaves of cooked cabbage, and a cup of water.

Domestic pets get better treatment than we got in prison. Those patients in the prison were left behind, just like abandoned animals. Life or death seemed to be an unimportant issue in the eyes of Japanese police.

I suffered complete loss of appetite, high fever, loss of hearing, vague consciousness, and a seemingly comatose state. I cannot recall how many months I spent in the isolation ward.

The patient lying beside me had his fever go down after some time and recovered his consciousness. As my consciousness also returned slightly, we could have a dialogue. He was a gentle and naive young Korean peasant. He had been imprisoned with an accused offense of evading forced labor by the Japanese colonial government. He was transferred to the general section of the prison.

My fever eventually came down, and my consciousness returned, as well as my hearing. I asked the prison guard to arrange my transfer. I was soon moved to a cell where five or six accused detainees were accommodated. The time was probably May 1945. I was glad to join relatively healthy-looking people.

One of those detainees was an old Japanese man who was an employee of a Japanese industrial company; he had been incarcerated after being accused of bribery. The other four or five people were all Koreans. One Korean was a member of the Hyeopdong Party and came from Kimhae, Kyeongnam Province. He was a young man of about thirty years of age who had graduated from a Japanese college.

I suddenly developed headache, chills, and fever at a certain time in the afternoon. Before my imprisonment, as a medical student, I occasionally suffered similar clinical signs and symptoms of malaria. Back then I treated myself with quinine anti-malarial drugs, since I had a medical history of malaria.

These clinical manifestations had previously occurred when I was in my hometown, Pohang City, Kyeongbuk Province, where my father practiced medicine for more than two decades. My father treated me with Salvarsan intravenous therapy and quinine sulfate medication.

Malaria responds symptomatically to anti-malarial medicine. The most important diagnostic test is a careful medical history, when a test with a blood smear preparation for the identification of malarial plasmodium is unavailable. Responsive anti-malarial drug therapy is also practically diagnostic for malaria. Relapse can occur in malaria.

There was no anti-malarial medicine in the prison. There was no way to get the drug. My physical condition was worsening daily with no hope of a cure. I could only suffer and endure the disease. Chronic malaria, if untreated, may lead to anemia, debility, and cachexia.

**Revelation in a Dream and Release from Prison**

I began to experience gradual recovery of my stamina from the weakened physical condition I had suffered due to severe typhus fever. One night, I dreamed a strange and unusual dream. An old man with a short haircut and wearing a gray Korean coat *(durumagi)* suddenly appeared in front of me in my dream. I had no time to think of other things. I fell to the ground face down and asked only one question. "When shall I be released from the prison?"

Instantly he answered my question by saying, "**The day is the thirty-first**."

With this answer, the old man disappeared, and at the same time I woke up from my dream. I felt the dream was so unusual. It was the dawn of a day in June 1945. The morning sunlight was coming through a high window of the prison wall. I could feel the cool air of early summer. I had never dreamed such an extraordinary dream in my life, especially one in which a specific date was revealed so clearly.

June had thirty days and July thirty-one days, and I speculated that the thirty-first day was surely the thirty-first day of July. I started looking forward to the end of July, the thirty-first day that had been revealed in my dream.

I whispered my dream to my Korean roommate who was a member of the Hyeopdong Party. After having listened to me, he told me that I would be better off awaiting that day, since my dream was so unusual and extraordinary.

After this event, days passed, and there were no special events or news with regard to my legal case.

Unexpectedly I suffered a recurrence of chronic malaria in the latter part of July. I became so sick and weak that I did not even think about the exceptional dream.

Time in the prison was passing day by day. Eventually the thirty-first day of July came. I was suddenly ordered to appear in the public prosecutor's office of Kyeongsung Court (Kyeongsung: Seoul). I met the Japanese prosecutor, Ei Kurokawa, who handled the Hyeopdong Party case.

He said to me, "For the last month, when I came home after finishing my daily work, your name suddenly came across my mind. I've kept thinking of you. I have been led to reconsider your case of the independence movement. I do not understand why I kept thinking about you every evening." He continued, "I have made up my mind today. There have been no cases in the past in which the accused detainees involved in any underground independence movement with suspected offenses against the security laws, like you students who joined the student organization of the independence movement, were all released. I have taken legal action so that all the other medical students except you have already been released from prison on probation. I had intended that only you among the students involved in the illegal independence movement should be continuously incarcerated and prosecuted in the upcoming trial."

He said, "However, although there have been no similar cases in the history of the prosecutor's office, I have made up my mind today, after one month of unusually difficult deliberation. I'm going to release you from prison today." His story and statements were unexpected.

He said to me at the end, "Go back to the prison today and wait."

It was incredible that I was actually released from the Seodemun Prison the night of July 31, 1945. The memory of that night has been unforgettable throughout my life.

Was it a coincidence? It was an experience beyond my comprehension. Since then, I have come to absolutely believe that the dream in June 1945 was a revelation from heaven. I had no way to know whether the old man who showed up in my dream was God, an angel, my ancestor, or Kwanseeum Bosal (Avalokitesvara). I still believe that God loves and protects my Korean friends and people who love peace and justice. I vividly recall the dream, even now after sixty years. I am deeply grateful for the grace of heaven.

## Release from Seodemun Prison to Korean Liberation on August 15, 1945

My release from Seodemun Prison by the order of the prosecutor Kurokawa on July 31, 1945 was unexpected. I was called to the main office of Seodemun Prison around 9:00 PM on July 31, 1945. There was a Korean police detective awaiting me in the office. I thought to myself that I might be taken again to the Seodemun Police Station for re-interrogation.

I got back my personal belongings, including my Korean thick winter clothes that I was wearing at the time of my arrest by the Japanese police in December 1944. I put on my clothes and followed the detective. I left the iron gate of Seodemun Prison. Unbelievably, it was exactly July 31, around 10:00 PM. I breathed cool, fresh air for the first time after nearly eight months of incarceration. I finally returned to my homeland and society. The sky was studded with innumerable stars that appeared to twinkle extraordinarily. Since then, I have clearly recalled that starlit night sky in my mind throughout my life.

The police officer told me for the first time that I was released from prison and left me alone in front of the prison gate. He disappeared in the dark street.

Then I went to a nearby Korean inn. After checking in, I went to a room. I went out to the central yard, where there was a well pump. Working at the well pump, I could get fresh water—as much as I wanted. I washed my face, hands, and feet. At that moment, it reminded me of prison life, where only a cup of water was available for washing one's face each day. I was overwhelmingly grateful for the limitlessly available underground water from the well pump.

It was hard to get to sleep that night because I had many thoughts of prison life and the future. In addition, attacks from biting bedbugs made me sleep much worse that night.

The next morning, I woke up and groomed. After breakfast, I left the inn. I breathed the summer morning air, full of hope. I enjoyed the sunlight and the blue sky. I got onto a streetcar at Seodemun.

I was standing in the streetcar, wearing white, Korean winter clothes made of thick cotton layers in the hot summer. I must have appeared strange-looking with my unusual winter apparel and pale, emaciated face; however, I was inwardly feeling joy.

I saw many passengers in the streetcar, mostly people going to work and school. I happened to see a student of Kyeongsung University from my medical school, wearing a square black cap and a black student uniform.

I threaded through the passengers and got close to him. I recognized him as one of my classmates, Byung Suhl Suh (now deceased). We were pleased to see each other. I told him I had been released last night. He was not involved in our student independence movement, and he had continued to attend the medical school during the period of my incarceration. He was one of my most respected classmates, an outstanding and promising student who knew many foreign languages.

I got off the streetcar at Keonji-Dong. I visited my classmate Sang Im Cha, who was one of those students arrested and released from the prison earlier than I had been. I told him of my release and my urgent need of anti-malarial treatment. Then his brother-in-law Dr. Hui Yeong Choi, of the Keonji Hospital where my friend Cha was a resident, treated me with Salvarsan intravenous therapy and quinine sulfate pills for my chronic malaria. My fever began to come down after the treatment. Slowly and gradually I recovered my health and strength. If I had not been released from prison on July 31 and had continued to be incarcerated, my physical condition would have gotten unimaginably worse.

The next day I went to Kyeongseong University's College of Medicine. I met a Japanese professor of pharmacology named Yoshida who was the chief of student affairs. He told me that I had been withdrawn from the school at the professors' meeting. I was not on the list of medical college students. Prof. Yoshida suggested that if I would like to come to school, I might come and work in the garden on the college grounds.

A few days later, I met Prof. Yoshida on the morning of August 15, 1945. He informed me of an important radio broadcast scheduled at noon. I waited and listened to the radio at 12:00 noon.

I heard clearly that Japan's Emperor Hirohito had announced his unconditional surrender to the Allied forces. I was overwhelmed with joy to hear of the Japanese surrender as a reality, even though we had anticipated Japanese defeat. I felt tremendous joy and hope to know that we, the Korean people, were liberated from the thirty-five-year-long Japanese colonial rule forever. We got back our freedom and the sovereignty of Korea. In addition, personally I would be freed of the expelled status from school and be able to go back to Kyeongseong University's College of Medicine.

I met with Prof. Yoshida again. He appeared unusually gloomy. He congratulated me on the Korean liberation and wished a bright future for us, the Korean people.

Outside the medical college grounds, Korean national flags, the Taegeug-Ki, were waving for the first time in my life. Korean people swarmed in the streets in celebration, shouting for joy, chanting, *"Manse,"* "Viva Korea," "Viva the Republic of Korea," and "Viva Ten Thousand Years, Liberation of Korean People." The shouts of joy were filling the high, blue sky.

We publicly expressed our deepest gratitude to the Allied forces that had fought for peace and justice around the globe, sacrificing their lives and bringing freedom and independence for the Korean people. Since then, August 15 has been celebrated as Independence Day.

During my eight months of imprisonment, I survived cruel treatment, torture, disease, and malnutrition, and now I was embraced in the bosom of our motherland, liberated by the victory of the Allied forces and the grace of heaven.

A few days later, my medical college classmates who had participated in the student independence movement of the Hyeopdong Party, some of whom had been imprisoned and had endured physical and emotional abuse and isolation behind bars for about six or eight months, as well as some of the other classmates who had fled and hidden in the countryside away from the school and had suffered hard lives, all returned to Kyeongseong University's (now Seoul National University) College of Medicine. We could now resume the study of medicine that we had been longing to pursue.

Countless Korean people who had worked hard with sweat and tears in factories, mines, and fields inside and outside the Korean peninsula, forced to work by the Japanese colonial government during the war, and who had been forcefully drafted into Japan's army, regained their freedom and rejoiced in the hope of reconstructing the Korean nation.

## Contemplation Relating to the Ideology of the Korean Liberation Hyeopdong Party (朝鮮民族解放協動黨)

As the Grand East Asia War (as World War II was called by the Japanese) perpetrated by Japan was growing fierce, the global circumstances surrounding the Korean peninsula were changing every day. At that time, some of our Korean students of the Kyeongseong University College of Medicine were highly inspired by the ideology of the Hyeopdong Party and joined its underground independence movement in 1944.

According to this ideology, it was anticipated that Japan's defeat would occur before long, and that World War II would end soon with the victory of the US-led alliance.

There would be an absence of a Korean government to take appropriate measures in the Korean peninsula. Using this opportunity, world superpowers would competitively struggle to encroach on the Korean homeland: the Soviet Union from the north, the United States and England from the south, and China from the west.

If we, the Korean people, allowed this to occur, Koreans would become their slaves. Therefore, all Korean people must unite, defend, and establish an independent Korean nation as a buffer zone among these competing world powers.

We intended to build a bright future with a free and independent Korea. Then we would found an ideal society on the basis of the ideology of the Hyeopdong Party.

In an ideal society, all citizens of the society would work without being exploited. The universe has both visible material and invisible order (law). Man has aspects of both body and mind. Therefore, economies, sciences, politics, religions, arts, sports, etc. that are composed of both the physical, material aspect and the mental, spiritual aspect will likewise tremendously develop and advance in the ideal society.

The ideology is comprehensive and progressive. It respects individual freedom and human rights.

I would like to describe several issues related to the ideology of the Hyeopdong Party, since the ideas below occurred to me while examining the basic thoughts of the party.

**1.** We must unite in order to regain autonomy and national sovereignty. We must be spiritually armed and overcome a period of confusion and disorder that might occur in Korea as a buffer zone.

**2.** We shall protect our constitution, written on the basis of the fundamental principle that guarantees human rights and freedom will be respected and upheld throughout the Korean peninsula. The people shall govern the country. The constitution will uphold the separation of the executive, the legislative, and the judiciary branches that have just and fair representation of individual citizens, on the basis that all citizens are equal before the law.

**3.** The economy is allowed to be built on free-market principles, and therefore a market-oriented economy is chosen, not a controlled, planned economy. Outstanding and gifted entrepreneurs will work together with a hard-working labor force, helping and sustaining each other mutually with brotherly love and unprecedented, admirable cooperation, and without exploitation between them.

Each person in the nation will work to his or her full capacity. The reward to each working person shall be guaranteed and reasonably provided.

The government shall make its utmost effort to establish the best policies to promote economic growth and create jobs. The government shall not be intrusive and will not unreasonably interfere in personal and business affairs.

Personal property is recognized and legally protected. We shall construct an ideal society throughout the country in which each citizen can pursue his or her own health, prosperity, and happiness. In contrast to this ideal society, in a communist-ruled society there exists heteronomous political and economical control by a minority power-holding class, actually a very small number of central communist members. It prohibits personal property that is the foundation of human economic actions as a driving force.

In addition, it emphasizes unreasonable equality in the economic structural force for hegemony and control, and unfair equality in distribution of profits, which indicates indiscriminate exploitation of the talented and more productive management people and entrepreneurs by inconsiderate, selfish, labor-oriented people with resentment and hatred of personal wealth, rather than free-market competition by means of upgrading efficiency and productivity.

This reduces motivation to work harder to increase productivity, which produces laziness, an inherent human weakness, and weakens willpower for productivity. The above-described factors eventually lead to worrisome economic collapse of the social economy. Therefore, a communist-ruled society is obviously undesirable.

In 1991, within eighty years after the 1917 communist revolution, the Soviet Union and the Eastern European communist countries tumbled and collapsed. It is quite clear that this historical fact proves the above theories are true and valid.

The government should make the utmost effort to establish policies that assist sound national economic development.

**4.** The national defense force must always be maintained and strengthened in order to preserve our free democratic nation and to meet the needs of national defense forever. Armed forces are not used to invade other countries but to preserve the sovereignty of Korea and human rights, and further to prevent invasion by terrorists.

If peaceful measures of diplomatic negotiation or political and economic sanctions were not successful, then the use of powerful armed forces would be justified to fight and annihilate invasions. Defeating any foreign invasions or illegal domestic revolts is necessary.

All free democratic nations of the world shall unite under the United Nations and prevent crimes of invasive wars (such as World War I and World War II, perpetrated by Hitler, Stalin, and Japanese imperialists) from recurring.

**5.** All Korean citizens are entitled to have sufficient food, clothing, housing, medical insurance, and the best education as their birthright.

Politicians shall endeavor to their fullest capacity to provide for the basic well-being of their constituents, to establish policies to provide living expenses to the elderly population, and to render assistance for unemployment. The government is obliged to implement these policies.

The government shall allocate the revenue from the best and most appropriate tax code system and provide funds for national education; medical insurance; strong defense; the executive, the legislative and the judiciary branches; scientific research; and so on.

The government should attempt to control deficit spending and avoid overtaxation, provide tax cuts whenever possible, and keep a balanced budget, and it is obliged to implement the most appropriate financial and economic policies.

**6.** National education is principally free. The government shall give opportunities for learning to all citizens. Young students can receive the highest education and professional skills in their fields of study as long as they have sufficiently qualifying talents and capabilities and will. Scholarships are implemented and available to those students for the above purpose within the scope of the national financial aid budget.

Teachers shall have the highest standards at each level of education.

Geniuses in any arenas of culture, science, engineering, technology, economy, music, art, education, and so forth shall receive encouragement and financial aid from the government and private sector so that they will be able to fully develop their gifted talents and abilities.

**7.** The Korean family system is a beautiful custom of the Orient. This custom will be respected and preserved. Confucianism, on which the family system is deeply founded, shall be taught to young people. The role of parents is very important in education about morality and human relationships.

**8.** When we understand the above-described ideology of the Hyeopdong Party and further achieve its expansion and development, expanded and developed ideologies will be so comprehensive and acceptable to Korean people that we may be able to think about the following issues:

a. Nationalism, racism, and communism have made meritorious contributions in the course of regaining the independence of Korea and ought to be recognized. However, when the Korean people have finally acquired Korea's independence, these ideologies are felt unnecessary to debate or to adhere to, and they could be abandoned eventually.

b. Extreme and selfish capitalism, conservatism, progressivism, and revolutionary idealism are likewise to be abandoned (Karl Polanyi, *The Great Transformation* [57]).

These ideologies would be fused and united into one desirable, ideal society. The ideal society is advancing toward a truly desirable human society that will be a society of love and compassion, sharing joy with others, and relieving the sadness of others. This might be called communal freedom and democracy.

**9.** If any individuals, small organizations, or any other countries repent their past mistakes or wrongdoings done from their ignorance and greed, and make proper compensation with a true apology, and come back to the side of communal freedom and democracy, they will be magnanimously treated, forgiven, and welcome to join our construction of the ideal society of well-being.

**10.** Government officials of each nation have the duty to teach the above-mentioned true ideology and to teach their own people the true history of their country without distorting facts in their history books.

## Preparatory School, Kyeongseong Imperial University

I was educated in elementary and high schools that were attended by only Korean students. The teaching staff consisted of both Korean and Japanese teachers. I was admitted to the preparatory school of the Kyeongseong Imperial University College of Medicine. Together with my Korean and Japanese classmates, I got an advanced college education.

I was surprised that the number of Korean students was only half that of my Japanese classmates. Children of Japanese people living in Korea as a minority occupied the majority of seats in our higher educational system. My second surprise was that the professors were all Japanese. When I advanced to medical college, there were also no Korean professors.

The awful fact that our Korean people were partly or totally excluded from the highest educational institution in Korea made me think that Japanese colonial policies were attempting to suppress Korean cultural development. In addition, the Japanese colonial government made it mandatory for Korean students to speak the Japanese language at school exclusively, in an attempt to wipe out our own Korean mother tongue.

The above-described injustices and unfair Japanese colonial policies in our highest educational institutions made me resentful and angry at Japanese colonial rule.

Whenever problems and arguments among students and racial discrimination in the school administration arose, my racial consciousness became stronger. Korean students spontaneously became unified.

There were two classes in each grade of the preparatory school; the students of the B Group were scheduled to advance to medical college after graduation. I recall now most clearly Chong Suhl Kim, the late Jung Jin Kim, and Sang Im Cha among my classmates.

These three Korean classmates were felt to have strong racial consciousness and to be patriotic. They spearheaded, vindicated, and encouraged Korean students whenever any friction arose between Korean and Japanese students. Chong Suhl Kim invited all of my Korean classmates to his home for a friendship dinner party. We had a great time. We emjoyed close friendship, firm solidarity, and wonderful entertainment.

One day at Kim's home, I met Woon Hyeong Lyuh (呂 運 亨), a patriot who had struggled for the independence movement his whole life and who unfortunately was assassinated by an unknown political opponent in 1945. I recall even now that he was a noble and greatly dignified man.

Another unforgettably beautiful memory is of the time my classmate Kwang Se Lim invited me to accompany him on a vacation to his hometown, Kaeseong, an old capital of the Koryo Dynasty. He was one of my medical school classmates who later participated in the independence movement of the Hyeopdong Party and was imprisoned.

I enjoyed seeing the beautiful scenery of nature surrounding Kaeseong City. I was overwhelmed to see the bloodstained, legendary stone bridge of Seonjuk Kyo (the "Good Bamboo" Bridge) on which my ancestor, Chung Mong Ju (鄭 夢 周, Po'eun 圃 隱, 1337–92) had shed his blood in 1392 when he was assassinated by a political opponent who plotted to topple the country. According to the legend, a bamboo tree suddenly arose from the ground beside the bridge at the time of his death, symbolizing his loyal righteousness. Since then the bridge has been named the Good Bamboo Bridge.

He served his country, Koryo, as a prime minister. He was a great scholar and statesman. He was also an outstanding diplomat, sent to China and Japan as a special envoy to smooth Korea's uncertain relationships with those countries.

His poem, best known as "The Fidelity Song" in Korea (translated by Jaihiun J. Kim) is below:

> Though I die and die again,
> though I did a hundred times,
> though my bones turn to dust
> and whether my soul exists or not,
> what could change this single-minded
> loyalty that glows toward my lord?

A legend says that his mother composed the following poem to warn her son against mixing with power-greedy political opponents (translated by Jaihiun J. Kim):

> White heron, do not venture
> into the valley where crows fight.
> The angry crows there will be
> jealous of your whiteness.
> I fear lest your clean-washed body
> be stained with black.

We were young and longing to explore an unknown world of literature, art, philosophy, and romance. We endeavored to learn the truth of life and the universe, and to find self-realization and so forth.

The majority of Korean students participated in soccer and basketball clubs. We enjoyed playing soccer or basketball in the daily one-hour gym class. I remember Jung Jin Kim's finest play in soccer as a champion. Korean students could have friendship and solidarity through our soccer and basketball play.

I occasionally joined the jujitsu club during the gym hour and played with Japanese classmates. One day there was a school jujitsu contest in which each class of the entire school would participate.

I do not understand why my Japanese classmates who were members of the jujitsu club chose me as the captain of my class team for the school jujitsu contest. I made up my mind to do my best to win if I participated in the contest. Each contestant was scheduled for one-on-one fights with his opponents. I did my best and won in all of my contests.

While I was returning home in a streetcar after the school jujitsu contest, a student one year my senior at the preparatory school approached me and said, "Hi. Today I watched the jujitsu contest. I was pleased to see you win the contest." He congratulated and encouraged me.

I have never forgotten this whole experience of the jujitsu contest in my life. It made me feel a kind of racial consciousness that gradually grew, combined with my religious beliefs from my middle school era onward.

## Kyeongbuk Middle School and High School

When I was a sophomore student at Kyeongbuk Middle School, my father got me a large series of more than twenty volumes of a Japanese-translated, updated Buddhist sutra. He recommended that I read the Buddhist scriptures.

Whenever I had free time in my middle-school and high-school days, I read them with great interest and deep joy. The teachings of Buddha Sakyamuni (558–479 BC) were fascinating and became the foundation of my early views on life and the world.

I was quite attracted to the great teachings. I made an oath to myself to do good things for my fellow people, first for my neighbors, the compatriots, and then for mankind, if possible.

My faith began to get stronger and deeper. I learned that our souls are immortal and indestructible. It is the highest virtue to sacrifice the body for others.

My father (the late Dr. Hwa Kee Chung, 鄭 華 基) told me that in his childhood he left his hometown, Yunil, Kyeongbuk Province, for Hanyang (Seoul) to study in middle school and high school after finishing elementary school. He attended Baejae School, which was affiliated with a Christian church. He worked as a self-supporting student for meals and school tuition.

My grandfather was the head of a farming family and also a scholar. He was a very righteous and decent man, a descendent of Chung Mong Ju, living in a small village. I heard the following remarkable stories about him. The *weonim* (a king-appointed administrator of a county in the Yi Dynasty) was committing wrongdoing in his county administration. My grandfather went to the county office, holding a lit lantern in daytime as a sign of warning to the *weonim,* the powerful administrator. When he was walking on the road, he did not look at or pay attention to pedestrians passing by. I certainly believe that my father received direct and indirect valuable teachings from my grandfather.

He told me an unforgettable, special story from his high-school days. One day he was sitting alone in his empty classroom and doing embroidery while the other classmates were playing on the playground in their gym hour. Chi Ho Yun (尹 致 昊, 1865–1946), who was affiliated with Baejae School and one of the earlier pioneers who had studied in the United States, happened to visit the school. He was a faithful Christian and came from a well-known family.

While he was looking at classrooms, he came across my father's room. He unexpectedly saw my father working on embroidery. He asked him, "Why don't you go out to the playground like the other students during gym hour?"

My father replied, "Sir, I am a self-supporting student with difficulties. I've got to work to earn bread and school tuition. I am doing embroidery. I can't spend time playing outside as the other students do."

Yun, who was associated with the Baejae Foundation and an active person for Christianity and education, seemed moved. He said, "Well, I understand you now. If you are a self-supporting student, you may come to my house and stay as a private tutor for my children."

My father gladly accepted his offer. Later he finished high school and fortunately even advanced to the Kyeongseong medical school through the financial aid of Chi Ho Yun. He graduated from medical school in 1922.

I was so pleased to hear his story during my childhood, and I thanked Chi Ho Yun for his generosity to my father. Chi Ho Yun was a patriot and is believed to be the person who wrote the Korean national anthem.

My father practiced medicine at my hometown, Pohang, Kyeongbuk Province, for more than four decades, treating patients, including Japanese patients. For a few years during his private medical practice, he went to Japan for residency training in internal medicine under the guidance of Dr. Inada (稲 田), a professor of medicine at the Tokyo Imperial College of Medicine. My parents took me with them to Japan. I remember that I made friends right away and played with Japanese neighbor kids in my preschool childhood.

I was born as a second son. My mother (the late Kwi Dol Chung, 鄭 貴 乭) was a gracious, warmhearted, and selfless mother. My parents loved their children. My father especially liked world literature, Korean and Chinese history, *Samkuk-Chi* (a famous Chinese history book written in Chinese characters), and Chinese poetry. He had believed in Christianity since his high-school days. He was also knowledgeable about Buddhism and Confucianism. I came to know Christianity, Buddhism, and Confucianism through my father's personal education.

I studied the bible myself in preparatory school. I studied Buddhism during middle school and high school.

My father told me of so many memorable and fascinating historical events in Korea. The most important story was about the great Korean admiral Yi Sun Shin (李 舜 臣, 1545–98) in the seven-year war of Imjin Wae Ran, the Japanese invasion of Korea (1592–8). Admiral Yi and national troops, together with righteous civilian soldiers and Buddhist monk volunteer warriors, fought bravely and decisively defeated the Japanese invading enemies. Only a few Japanese soldiers and sailors could flee to Japan. This famous war story is recorded in both Korean and Japanese history books.

Admiral Yi fought and won battles against Japanese fleets, using *kobukson,* or "turtle ships," that were designed and built by him and that were the world's first ironclad ancestors of modern warships. According to Rick Beyer's *The Greatest War Stories Never Told* [8], the turtle ships were completely covered with iron plating and spikes that prevented enemies from boarding the ships and made Japanese guns and flaming arrows useless. The turtle ships accommodated up to twenty-six cannons in portholes made in the sides of the ships.

Joong Kun An was a patriot under Japanese annexation and colonial rule. On March 1, 1919, the Korean Declaration of Independence was read publicly in Pagoda Park in Seoul, and Koreans protested against Japanese colonial rule throughout the country. Many of those Korean compatriots were imprisoned and killed by Japanese police. Korea commemorates March 1 as Independence Movement Day.

I am respectful and grateful to those of our ancestors who laid down their lives for the country, fighting foreign invasions.

## Thoughts on Japanese Imperial Colonial Policy

Arrogant and greedy Japanese foreign policy perpetrated several unjust invasive wars against Japan's neighboring countries, Korea, Manchuria, China, and many other Asian countries around the Pacific Ocean; Imjin Wae Ran, the Japanese invasion of Korea (1592–8); and annexation and colonial rule of Korea (1910–45).

Atrocities committed by Japanese invaders must be clearly recorded in human history. Merciless torture and abuse of human rights should be absolutely condemned in human society.

The leader of the Hyeopdong Party, Jong Baek Kim (金 宗 伯, San Hae, 山 海) was imprisoned and unfortunately died in Seodemun Prison in 1945. He was an unknown patriot who fought against Japanese colonial rule and tried to save Korea's oppressed people from an extremely distressing state.

Hopefully his ideology, described above, will last generations in Korea. He will go down as a patriot in Korean history.

There are political movements even now in Japan that are trying to distort their history textbooks for young people in order to justify the past Japanese colonial rule of Korea and the invasion of Asian countries in World War II. These phenomena are really bad. I hope that wise and honest Japanese people will examine themselves and make efforts to eradicate those ugly, wrong actions. I wish that Japanese people would make efforts to contribute to the peace of the East Asia and the whole world.

Despite my insufficient talent in writing, I have endeavored to write this long letter in order to clarify the truth and to answer your questions that you asked in your letter of 10/28/2005. I have also tried to elucidate some seemingly pertinent subjects.

I love our homeland as well as my adopted country, the United States.

I have limited descriptions of my experiences up until August 15, 1945, the day of Korean liberation, following your advice in your letter.

I pray from the bottom of my heart that you be healthy and able to continue your good work for the country.

I am including a poem by Lee Baek and a German poem that I recite sometimes when I recall our yearning, justice-minded, young, and romantic school days and my homeland, now that we who experienced stormy lives are in our eighties.

Lee Baek's poem

牀 前 明 月 光
疑 是 地 上 霜
擧 頭 望 明 月
低 頭 思 故 鄉

Goethe's poem
Kennst du das Land, wo die Zitronen blühn,
Im dunkeln Laub die Gold-Orangen glühn,
Ein sanfter Wind vom blauen Himmel weht,
Die Myrte still und hoch der Lorbeer steht,
Kennst du es wohl?
　　　　Dahin! Dahin
Möcht ich mit dir, o mein Geliebter, ziehn.

I hope we can continue our communication when time allows. When you visit the United States next year, I would be grateful if you came and saw my family.

Yours sincerely,
Sung Jang Chung

## Recommended Books for Grandchildren to Read

1. The bible
2. Buddhist scripture
3. Classics of Confucianism
4. Dalai Lama, *The Universe in a Single Ato*m. Morgan Road Books, New York, 2005.
5. Dalai Lama, *365 Dalai Lama: Daily Advice from the Heart.* HarperCollins, London, 2001.
6. Kader Asmal, David Chidester, and Wilmot James, *Nelson Mandela in His Own Words.* Little, Brown and Company, New York, 2003.
7. Benjamin Pogrund, *Nelson Mandela.* Blackbirth Press, Farmington, Michigan, 2003.
8. Jimmy Carter, *Our Endangered Values.* Simon & Schuster, New York, 2005.
9. Robert T. Oliver, *A History of the Korean People in Modern Times: 1800 to the Present.* University of Delaware Press, Newark, Delaware, 1993.
10. Richard Rutt, *James Scarth Gale and his History of the Korean People.* Seoul Computer Press, Seoul, 1972.
11. *Korea Today.* Monthly Photo Journal, October 1988.

## — CHAPTER 3 —

## My Life in the Korean War

### 1. Outbreak of the Korean War

In the early morning of Sunday, June 25, 1950, the Republic of Korea (ROK) was suddenly invaded by North Korean enemy forces. North Korea's Kim Il Sung, with Soviet Union leader Joseph Stalin's backing, had secretly plotted and eventually started an atrocious war with the intention of overthrowing the Republic of Korea by force and taking over the entire Korean peninsula, enslaving everyone under communism.

North Korea launched a ferocious preemptive war against South Korea at a time when the ROK government was totally unprepared to counterattack and crush the North Korean armed attack. ROK armed forces were overrun by the North Korean incursion. Lightly armed ROK forces and the government were forced to retreat by the advancing, ruthless North Korean forces equipped with modern Russian weapons (Leif A. Gruenberg, *Defining Moments: The Korean War* [36]; Max Hastings, *The Korean War* [39]).

ROK forces, government officials, and civilians hastily retreated toward the south, passing the bridge over the Han River.

Citizens of the capital, Seoul, were in stunned confusion and in a chaotic situation by the time North Korean forces reached the outskirts of the city. The Han River bridge was destroyed by explosives after ROK forces and high-ranking government officials passed south on June 26 and 27. Many Seoul citizens lost opportunities to flee Seoul and experienced the capital falling to North Korean forces on June 28, 1950.

Countless Seoul citizens were killed and kidnapped by ruthless North Korean soldiers, police agents, and Communist Party members during the communist occupation. Many South Korean youths were conscripted into the North Korean army.

South Korean president Syngman Rhee (李承晚, 1875–1965) pleaded with the United States to provide urgent aid in fighting the North Korean communist aggressors. President Harry Truman of the United States, a nation friendly to South Korea, denounced North Korean aggression of South Korea by force. After the UN Security Council unanimously passed a resolution to denounce the lawless aggression of North Korea and to provide military aid to South Korea, the US-led United Nations forces, with General Douglas MacArthur as their supreme commander, came to South Korea to block the advance of the North Korean forces and to save the Republic of Korea. The UN forces and ROK forces bravely fought fierce battles to restore international peace and security.

I lost a good chance to take refuge to the south. I was one of the citizens of Seoul who remained in the capital city. I continued to work at the Department of Physiology of the Seoul National University College of Medicine.

## 2. Forced Transportation to the North and Experiences in the Early Part of the Korean War in North Korea

After the outbreak of the Korean War, I went daily to the Department of Physiology as a graduate student.

One day, a bus was dispatched by the Ministry of Public Health and parked on the campus in front of the building of the basic medical departments of the College of Medicine. Our medical staff and students received an unexpected order, from an unknown Communist Party superior office, to board the bus immediately. The destination was untold. The purpose of the bus ride was also unknown to us. Scores of medical staff members had to get on the bus. The bus went to the office of the Ministry of Public Health.

An apparent Communist Party member showed up and told us, "Comrades, you are going to be transported to the north, to Pyongyang." He went on to say, "Be aware that in Pyongyang, you will be scheduled to be dispatched to different medical institutions in North Korea."

This was a surprise order from the Communist regime. Later the bus promptly left the building of the Ministry of Public Health and transported us to North Korea. We arrived at a school building campus in Pyongyang after several hours' drive. In a classroom, we met a group of South Korean physicians who had been forcibly transported to North Korea ahead of us. Dr. Myung Bok Lee, a professor of anatomy at Seoul College of Medicine, was among them.

Physicians who had arrived before our group were moved away to various regions of North Korea that were unknown to us. A new group of seven South Korean physicians, including me, was transported by truck to Wonsan and Hamhung. Byung Sul Suh, one of my medical school classmates, got off the truck at Wonsan. (Dr. Suh became a professor of parasitology and later the dean of the Seoul College of

Medicine after returning to South Korea. He has since passed away.) I and the other remaining doctors were moved to Hamhung City.

My group of physicians was ordered to work at Hamhung Provincial Hospital. I was assigned to the Department of Medicine. The other five physicians were assigned to work at different departments. The North Korean medical staff working at the hospital were the faculty of Hamhung Medical School at the same time. I practiced medicine with the chief of the Department of Medicine, treating general civilian outpatients. In the evenings after work, I stayed at a small boarding house with the five other physicians in my group.

Inpatients were treated by other physicians. Those inpatients included both North Korean civilians and soldiers.

Air raids involving machine-gun strafing by U.S. fighter planes and bombing by scores of B-29 bombers in a formation were daily getting more severe. Each time siren signals of an air raid ceased, hospital relief teams in trucks were dispatched to the bombed areas. We performed first-aid rescue treatment on wounded civilians.

Since the formidable bombings were at intervals in a wave pattern, the rescue team encountered unexpected bombing by the B-29s. We would lie prone on the ground, hearing the *shh* sound of the falling bombs in the air. Whenever we heard an explosion roar, we realized we were still alive. We frequently heard the *shh* sounds of falling bombs in the air above our heads.

One day, a North Korean army major showed up in our hospital and made all of the South Korean physicians gather in the playground of the hospital. He said, "Comrades, you have come from South Korea and have been treating our North Korean wounded and sick soldiers. Your activities in your medical service show insufficient efforts and insincerity." He went on to say, "Although this would deserve being shot to death as a reactionary act, you will be excused this one time. I urge you to be very faithful and sincere in your medical service."

He accused us without any substantial proof of wrongdoing in our medical service. He did not explain any concrete evidence for his allegation. We had no idea where he'd gotten such information. I still recall this unthinkable and inhumane event.

On another day, a few South Korean physicians and I were walking on a road near the hospital building. We unexpectedly met Shin Kyun Hwang, MD, who was one of my medical school classmates. I gladly greeted him. He was in a North Korean army uniform and was a major. He simply responded with a light blinking of his eyes as an apparent greeting without any other expression or words of joy. He walked away without stopping and disappeared from my sight. He seemed to be in a hurry. I was very stunned and saddened. I could not understand his behavior. I stopped walking and stayed there for a while.

He and I were especially close friends. We attended the same schools together, the Seoul Medical Preparatory School and the Seoul College of Medicine. After graduation from the College of Medicine, he got a job as a teaching assistant at the Department of Physiology of Ehwa Women's Medical College and majored in physiology. I entered Seoul National University Graduate School and majored in physiology and at the same time got a job as a teaching assistant at the Department of Physiology of Seoul Women's Medical College.

The two of us would meet at the Seoul College of Medicine's physiology department every Saturday afternoon. We studied differential and integral calculus. Each of us studied one chapter of the textbook and tried to solve ten to fifteen exercise problems at the end of the chapter each week. We discussed and solved the problems with questions and answers when we met on Saturday. It was an especially enjoyable math seminar.

After studying math, we played a violin duet. Shin Kyun Hwang took violin lessons in his childhood. His violin playing was exceptionally beautiful. We really enjoyed our Saturday afternoon math and music. Besides, both of us were awarded a prize by the German ambassador at the commencement when we graduated from the Seoul Medical Preparatory School.

He left a few months before the outbreak of the Korean War. His whereabouts were unknown to me.

We were dear friends with a special past. After I met Hwang in North Korea and he seemed to have abandoned our friendship, I could not fathom his behavior, although the Korean War was causing rapidly changing circumstances in the Korean peninsula.

I could not help thinking that the North Korean Communist government seemed to have changed my genuine, respectable, and outstanding friend Hwang into an apparently different person. My experience that day lives in my mind as an unforgettable memory.

The North Korean doctor who was the chief of the Department of Medicine was also a professor of medicine at Hamhung Medical School. I asked him a question concerning freedom of individual travel in North Korea. He replied, "I have not been more than ten miles outside of Hamhung City since I got my present job. Free individual travel is prohibited in North Korea without permission of the Communist superior officials." North Korean society seemed to be an inconvenient society that the Communist Party thoroughly controlled. According to his explanation, sick workers at factories could not be absent from their factories without a doctor's certificate of necessity of rest due to illness. The chief of medicine advised me not to issue a medical certificate of required rest without thorough consideration. We would get in trouble otherwise, with legal disciplinary punishment, if the government supervisor noticed it. There was a case in which a physician was imprisoned because of this.

There seemed to exist an unspoken struggle between doctor and patient. I felt strong compassion for sick workers.

General civilians were required to attend a scheduled lecture by the Communist Party after work in the evening for indoctrination in the ideology of communism. They were actually deprived of their free time even after work.

They absolutely could never criticize the North Korean government or the Communist Party in public places. They were allowed only to obey the orders of the Communists and act in compliance with the given orders.

In the daytime, whenever the air raid siren was heard, we had to stop medical service work and immediately seek refuge in an air-raid shelter. In those days, the circumstances during daylight hours did not allow medical staff to practice medical service activities, because US air raids were so frequent.

I thought often of the well-being of my parents at my hometown far away in the south. I also thought of my lover, who was in the south beyond the battlefields. I waited day by day, eagerly looking forward to meeting them as a free person when the Korean War ended.

### 3. Revelation in a Dream, Escape from North Korea, and Return to South Korea

One night, probably late in September 1950, I dreamed a strange dream. At the beginning of the dream, I saw a wall calendar with a black printed number of the date on white, rectangular paper. The number was crystal clear: **13**. That seemed to indicate that the thirteenth day would be an especially important and critical day. The calendar then disappeared, and subsequently I saw a night scene. In the darkness, I was walking in one direction with other people in a line.

I looked around both sides of the road. There was a flowing river on the left side and a mountain on the right side. While walking, I told a nearby nurse, "If we pass the thirteenth day, we will survive and have good days ahead. Let's be patient. We have hope."

The nurse who walked beside me appeared glad to hear me say it. After talking to the nurse, I woke up. I felt that the day would be the coming October 13. I awaited especially the thirteenth day of the next month, October. I believed that if I passed October 13 without any difficult events, I would have good days thereafter.

There was a good reason why I believed the extraordinary dream. In 1944, Korea was under the suppressive Japanese colonial government. I was a medical student of Keijo Imperial University College of Medicine. I joined a student underground organization for Korea's independence movement (the Hyeopdong Party). The movement was detected by Japanese police. I was arrested in December 1944. After interrogation and torture in the police station, I was imprisoned in Sudaemun Prison in Seoul. I had a specific dream in June 1945 similar to that in Hamhung in September 1950; it revealed a certain date of my release from prison (see chapter 2). The foretold date proved to be true. I have since believed that the dream in prison was a revelation from heaven. I thought that it was very rare to dream a specific date in a dream; therefore, I believed that the dream in North Korea was a second dream revelation in my life.

The next morning I told my dream to my South Korean physician colleagues. They listened to me and said that the dream seemed to be a strange one. They seemed to believe my dream as I did, with little doubt, at least apparently to me. We agreed that we would be better off waiting for October 13. They told some North Korean physicians and nurses that October 13 was Dr. Chung's birthday, but they kept my dream secret. They told me later that they would await October 13 together with me.

I don't remember reading any newspapers in North Korea. True news seemed to be completely blocked. In North Korean society, freedom of the press, including news reports concerning the Korean War, seemed to be prohibited.

The great historical battle at Inchon, including the landing by UN and ROK forces on September 15, 1950; recapture of the capital, Seoul, on September 27–8; crossing the 38th parallel on October 9; and the northward advance of UN and ROK forces, were totally unknown to South Korean physicians in Hamhung (Leif A. Gruenberg, *Defining Moments: The Korean War* [36]; Max Hastings, *The Korean War* [39]).

One day a North Korean nurse working at the Department of Medicine confided to me that she was listening to South Korean radio news secretly at home every night. I assumed that she trusted me because I came from South Korea and was doing medical service. She said, "According to the radio news, UN and ROK forces have advanced to Wonsan." She also told me that they would be near Hamhung in a few days. What she said was startling news to me. The day she confided this to me was probably around October 11, 1950.

She also said that many North Korean people resent the North Korean government, and that citizens felt that they were under surveillance by other citizens unknown to them. It seemed to South Korean observers that a secret spy network was spread throughout the society, and that spies might submit secret reports to the Communist Party.

When I heard this from the nurse, I was shocked and found it hard to believe. The North Korean people seemed to live in an uneasy society. Even the traditional family system might be broken in extreme cases that South Koreans could not imagine. If a family member became a Communist Party member, it might bring trouble among the family.

Based on what I witnessed personally in North Korean society, the communities seemed to be uneasy, and the people seemed to live in constant fear.

Complete control of lighting was implemented at night, so that the community was lacquer-black dark. I often opened a window of the classroom (in daytime it was used as an outpatient clinic) to see the night scene. I could see black-looking mountains under the starlit sky. I contemplated the battlefields.

*When UN forces and ROK forces advance north and reach Hamhung City, how should I act? What kinds of situations will arise if street fighting takes place in the city?* Whenever I thought of these possible circumstances in the war, I used to recall my extraordinary dream, which I felt was a special revelation not only to me but also for my South Korean peace-and-justice-loving physician colleagues. I looked forward to October 13.

October 10 and 11 passed. According to the secret information given me by the nurse, UN and ROK forces were supposed to be advancing near the city of Hamhung. As I recognized daily changes in situations on the battlefield on the basis of the secret information, I began to feel strongly a strange wonder; that is, a religious joy, because I felt that my dream appeared to be becoming a reality in terms of the date and the war situation. The thought crossed my mind that we might see a true phase of the universe that would transcend the specific time phases of the past, present, and future, when the great mind behind the far, dark-appearing mountains of nature would fuse into one mind with the little, clear minds residing within our small bodies.

In the early morning of October 12, prior to sunrise, an emergency signal was delivered to us in the darkness. All hospital staff members were ordered to get up and gather in the playground. At this moment, I acted together with a North Korean doctor accidentally in the darkness. We guessed that UN and ROK forces had reached the outskirts of Hamhung City. We were feeling tension. A fierce fight in the city was anticipated. We might fight at the battle lines with guns and bayonets under command of the Communist Party.

We made up our minds to seek refuge. We thought that we should flee Hamhung City. We hid in an air-raid shelter, where we stayed for about half an hour. There was no news, and it was so quiet outside. The North Korean doctor said to me, "The situation is strange. I want to go to my house in the city rather than stay here." He was about to leave. Since I had no place to go, I left the shelter without any special destination; I just followed him.

I said to him, "Hello, I would like to go to your house to seek refuge too. Do you mind?" He accepted my wish and told me that I should hurry up and follow him.

We scrambled hastily without being noticed by others leaving the hospital. We soon got to the North Korean doctor's house. His mother-in-law was at his house alone. I was introduced to her. I could take shelter at his home. My environment was abruptly changed so much.

About one hour later, the North Korean doctor told me, "Dr. Chung, the present circumstances are strange, and it is so quiet outside. I am going to the hospital. I want to find out the real situation. I'll be back. You stay here."

I agreed with his opinion. I replied, "I will wait here. Please go ahead."

While I was waiting, I read a Korean philosophy book called *Jeong Yeok* (正 易, *Right Changes*) that I carried with me. While I was reading, I thought of my special dream again. *Today is October 12,* I thought.

*The date revealed in the dream was October 13. It seems to me that I am acting one day earlier.*

The above idea suddenly occurred to me. At that time the North Korean doctor came back home and told me that the entire hospital's staff members were supposed to evacuate the hospital and to retreat north the evening of the next day, October 13, following the instructions of the Communist person responsible for the hospital.

I was truly surprised to hear this news, because the day we were scheduled to retreat north perfectly coincided with the date of October 13 that I had dreamed. So I changed my mind. I went back to the hospital with the North Korean doctor.

The South Korean physicians who were gathered in formation at the hospital campus were all stunned to see me coming back to the hospital. They said to me, "Dr. Chung, where have you been? We have been worried about you very much, because we didn't see you."

My South Korean physician colleagues were glad to see me. We were concerned for each other and had gone through life-or-death hardships together. We were just like brothers.

The gathered hospital staff members were dismissed. We awaited the next evening, October 13.

On the night of October 12, I opened the window of the classroom as before. I saw the dark night scene of nature outside. I felt especially that night a very close and dear feeling for the far, black mountains. I realized that the special dream was transforming into a reality. I felt my heart beating strongly.

The great mind behind the mountains, the creator god, became one with my little human mind. Immeasurable joy mixed with wonder was springing in my bosom. I began to believe strongly in heaven's grace and help. At that moment I experienced truly a religious ecstasy: Buddhist rapture.

The next day was finally October 13, the day I had been waiting for. In the evening, the entire staff of the Hamhung Provincial Hospital gathered on the playground of the hospital campus, following the order of the Communist person in charge. Scores of North and South Korean physicians, nurses, and non-medical staff members started to retreat north on foot in a formation of lines and groups, leaving the hospital and the city of Hamhung behind.

I got out of the Hamhung City for the first time. All of the hospital personnel were walking in lines on the dark road. I looked at the surrounding natural scene while I was walking. The Chongjin River was on my left side, and mountains were on my right. It was an amazing event. The night scene was just like the landscape that I had dreamed a few weeks previously. The coincidence of the dream and the reality was unbelievably extraordinary, beyond expression, and it convinced me that the special dream was a revelation from heaven.

I spoke to a nurse who was beside me, as I had in my dream. "Hello. If we pass tonight, the thirteenth day, we will be free. Let's be patient tonight. We have good days from tomorrow."

I did not tell my dream. I talked similarly in reality as I had in my dream. I felt inexpressible joy and hope while I was walking.

The scene and experience in reality on that night of October 13, 1950, together with the extraordinary dream of revelation, have been living ever since in my mind as invaluable memories for more than fifty years of my life.

We reached the playground of an elementary school in a village in the north around midnight, after walking scores of miles. We were told to take a temporary rest there.

At that time, we six South Korean physicians determined to take advantage of this opportunity to flee toward the south. We promised that each person would go back to Hamhung and gather at Dr. Myung

Hak Kim's surgical hospital in the city. We left separately in groups of two.

My partner and I began to walk toward the south along ridges between rice fields in the dark night. About one hour later, we heard a dog barking, which meant the presence of a nearby village, and this made us tense. We had to avoid any villages.

We suddenly heard someone approaching in the darkness. When we got close to them, we found another group of two South Korean physicians who had left the school at the same time as our group did. They joined us, and we continued to walk.

There was a straw-thatched peasant house with a dim light in the field. We asked whether we could rest for a short time at their home. The owner of the house politely declined these unknown visitors in the late night. We decided to continue to walk despite being so tired.

The sun rose in the morning. We had to pass in front of a police branch office, but we were able to pass nervously without any troubles. After a short while, we stopped by another peasant house in the field. A few family members were having breakfast, sitting around a table. The farm family shared their breakfast with us after we identified ourselves as physicians. We had breakfast thankfully. One of the doctors gave the few bags of sugar we had—our entire supply—to them. We expressed our sincere appreciation and left the farmer's house.

I recollect the farmer's family even now. They treated us, unknown visitors whom they had met for the first time, to warm meals, despite their hardship in the fierce war. I was deeply moved by their kindness and great love given to hungry travelers passing by. I was so grateful to them. It is really sad that there has been no way to visit again and express my thanks to them.

Our group of four physicians continued our forced march. We encountered apparent refugees heading south. Getting close to them, they turned out to be two South Korean physicians, one North Korean physician who had hid with me in an air-raid shelter on October 12, several North Korean nurses of the Hamhung Provincial Hospital, and one North Korean army officer wearing hospital inpatient clothes who was a patient at the same hospital—seven or eight people all together. They had left Hamhung on the preceding day and retreated north with our group. They joined us, making a total of eleven or twelve people. We all continued to walk south.

The date was October 14, 1950. The road was the same one that all of the hospital staff members had taken to retreat north on foot the previous night. Littering both sides of the road were numerous dead bodies of North Korean soldiers killed on the battlefields and civilians killed by bombings, artillery shells, and machine-gun strafing. The scene of carnage was terrible.

Countless retreating North Korean foot soldiers in formation, their rifles on their shoulders, straggling soldiers, and civilian refugees were on the road, heading north. Among the crowd of people, ours was the only group—a strange-looking minority— making its way to the south, in the opposite direction.

The Chongjin River was flowing on the right, and mountains were on the left. We saw North Korean troops stationed at a location far ahead of us. A guard with a bayonet-fixed rifle was standing on the road in front of the troops. The area that we had to pass looked fierce and brutal. We moved toward the last front line of the Korean War that our group had to pass through.

I asked my senior physician, Dr. Won Kyu Suh, who was the instructor of pharmacology at the Seoul College of Medicine, to go in front of our group. He declined and advised me to go ahead of us. No one wanted go in front, leading us. We were co-patriots who shared a life-or-death fate like brothers and sisters.

I thought to myself about this difficult situation. When I recalled the special dream of revelation that I had dreamed in the previous month, and the fact that I had acted in reality similarly to my actions in that dream, joy, faith, and courage spontaneously arose and filled my heart. I would not die here, because heaven was helping me. There would surely be some job that I would be obliged to perform in the future. I had unshakable religious faith and peace of mind. My fear was totally gone. There were no other choices. I made up my mind to go ahead of us, for the sake of our group.

Alone, I went close to the North Korean rifleman. The guard questioned me as expected. "Comrade, where are you going?"

The following words came out smoothly and uninterrupted from my mouth, without my thinking in advance. "Yes, I am a physician working at the Hamhung Provincial Hospital. Those people over there are physicians and nurses working together at the same hospital. Here is my ID card."

After showing my I.D. card, I continued to speak. "As a matter of fact, all of the hospital staff members of the Hamhung Provincial Hospital evacuated the hospital yesterday and retreated north. There is some medical equipment and supplies left at the hospital. We are going back and will bring them with us."

My statements appeared natural. I answered with a calm attitude. The guard stared at my face, and then scanned from my feet to the top of my head.

He appeared to trust my answer and attitude, in my judgment. He allowed me and all of my group to pass the guard line uneventfully. I had no doubt of heaven's help when got the guard's permission.

I turned back to our group and waved. "Come here all together, please. The guard has allowed us to pass and advance south."

Responding to my call, my senior and junior physicians, the North Korean doctor and nurses, and the wounded North Korean army officer showed joy in their faces and came hastily toward me. We all safely passed the most dangerous front line.

We resumed walking until dark. We sought refuge in the tunnel of a water gate on the quiet bank of the Chongjin River. We heard many roars of exploding shells of artillery fire, noises made by retreating North Korean tanks, and the staccato firing of small arms. We went occasionally out of the tunnel and saw artillery lightning and gun flashes in the night sky.

A fierce battle took place on the outskirts of Hamhung City on the night of October 14. The next day, October 15, the bright dawn came. The surrounding area became so quiet and calm. The battle appeared to have ceased. Some of our group got out of the tunnel and found it very quiet outside. We judged that the North Korean forces had broken and fled north. We felt some complacency and ease. We decided to leave the tunnel and go back to Hamhung City.

On October 15, we visited Dr. Myung Hak Kim's private hospital in the city. We greeted him with great pleasure. We stayed at his home for a few days. We received warm hospitality from Dr. and Mrs. Kim. We did not know how to express our deepest thanks to them for their generosity and friendship.

Dr. Kim was a renowned surgeon, a professor of surgery at Hamhung Medical School, and the chief of the Department of Surgery at Hamhung Provincial Hospital. He performed surgeries daily on North Korean civilians and soldiers who were wounded by bombings and gunfire in the war.

He saved countless human lives. Anyone who knew of his outstanding medical knowledge and surgical skills as well as his decent character respected him very much. He used to get up at 3:00 every morning and start his daily work faithfully. He was a hard worker too.

His two-story concrete hospital building was temporarily utilized as the ROK surgeons' office of the Third and Capital Divisions. One army surgeon was a medical classmate of one physician of our group. They greeted each other with much pleasure. The surgeon told our doctor that he was supposed to fly back to Seoul by helicopter the next day. He offered our doctor a helicopter flight with him, returning to Seoul; however, our doctor declined his kind offer. The reason for his refusal was that he could not go to Seoul alone, leaving the rest of our group who had shared life-or-death hardships together. I was so moved by the warm friendship shown by our doctor when I heard this story later.

We spent several days at Dr. Kim's house safely, without any inconveniences. Then we went to Wonsan by army truck after we bid farewell to Dr. and Mrs. Kim.

I unexpectedly met a classmate from Pohang Elementary School on a pier of Wonsan Harbor. He was a naval officer of an ROK submarine. He greeted me so gladly. He advised me to accept his suggestion that he would take me to my hometown, Pohang, in his submarine. At that moment, the thought of the doctor in my group came across my mind. I declined his kind suggestion of a good chance to return to South Korea, in order to act together with our group of physicians.

The next day, a UN LST ship transported hundreds of North Korean prisoners of war from Wonsan Harbor to South Korea. Our group of South Korean physician refugees boarded the LST ship together and later finally arrived at Pusan Harbor.

I happened to meet a student of Seoul Women's Medical College. One physician of our group and I stayed at the student's home one night, with much thanks. I went to Taegu and met my brother's family. After that, I finally returned to my hometown, Pohang.

I greeted my parents, who had worried so much about me, with no communications or news since the outbreak of the Korean War. My parents welcomed me, who had gone through various risks and fled North Korea, finally returning safely to the Republic of Korea.

I thanked God from the bottom of my heart for his grace and help.

## 4. Service as a Military Surgeon of the Republic of Korea Air Force

1. I got a job at the Taegu National Relief Hospital, where Dr. Ku Choong Chung was administrator. Dr. Myung Su Oh, associate professor of surgery at the Seoul College of Medicine, was the chief of surgery in the relief hospital.

I worked at the hospital under the direction of Dr. Oh. I diligently provided medical treatment to wounded civilian and North Korean refugee inpatients. I also served as an assistant surgeon in the operating room, to my full capacity.

2. In June 1953, I volunteered for the Republic of Korea Air Force. I was commissioned as an Air Force lieutenant and appointed as the chief of the First Section at the Air Force Aeromedical Institute of the Air Force Hospital in Masan, Kyungnam Province. I came to Seoul, where the institute was relocated later. Colonel Jae Wi Choi became the chief of the institute in Seoul.

3. On July 4, 1953, I got married to Dr. Kwang Jun Lee (李 廣田), who was in residency training in obstetrics and gynecology after her graduation from the Seoul Women's Medical College (now the Korea Medical College). The wedding ceremony was held at the chapel of

the Korean Cheondokyo (a Korean indigenous religion). My father-in-law was Dan Lee (李 團), who was the person responsible for the Cheondokyo and at one time the chairman of the Republic of Korea Association of Religions. I had known her for six years, before the outbreak of the Korean War. Before our marriage, we did research experiments together under the direction of Dr. Bong Han Kim, the chairman of the Department of Physiology at the Seoul Women's Medical College.

We had been separated due to the North Korean invasion; I was in North Korea and Miss Lee in South Korea. We had heard nothing from each other during the early period of the war. After my return from North Korea, we could finally be married. We have been married for more than fifty years. We are so grateful to God.

4. On July 27, 1953, the armistice ending the Korean War was signed at Panmunjom in a military confrontation [36]. In the three-year war that started with the North Korean incursion into South Korea, a fierce civil war in the Korean peninsula, with the loss of countless human lives and devastation of cities and villages, ceased with an uneasy, fragile truce; at any moment, war could break out again. The demilitarized zone along the 38th parallel that had brought division and tragedy from its beginning still remains, dividing Korea into South and North Korea.

There is yet no peaceful reunification under the United Nation's supervision. The alliance between the Republic of Korea and the United States with an American-Korean defense pact deters another Korean War in the current circumstances of mutual distrust, underlying hostility, and fear in the Korean people.

5. In November 1956, I attended the U.S. Far East Air Force Fifth Medical Conference in Baguio, Philippines. I presented my research paper on g-force (acceleration). After the conference, Major General

Niese, who was the surgeon general of the U.S. Far East Air Force, and Colonel John Stapp, who presided at the presentation of my article, flew to Seoul in order to see our Air Force Aeromedical Institute. After their inspection tour, they offered me a collaborative research position in the United States Air Force. However, I had to decline their special offer, since my sick father stayed at my home in Seoul at that time.

Colonel Stapp was a scientist famous for his research work related to the medical effects of g-force. The U.S. Congress adopted his research work results and enacted safety-belt laws. American people are required by law to use a safety belt while driving any motor vehicle. Safety-belt use has been reducing the risk of death and saving many lives every year since.

6. I was discharged as Air Force major of the Republic of Korea Air Force reserve in August 1958. After discharge, I was appointed chairman of the Department of Physiology at the Catholic Medical College in Seoul. I dedicated myself to medical student education and research.

## 5. Contemplation Regarding North Korean Communist Society

Facts that I witnessed and personally experienced in North Korea after my forced transportation were described above. Several issues that I feel when I reexamine North Korean communist society on the basis of these facts are as follows:

1. The North Korean communists do not recognize individual freedom and human rights. Communists do not place values on human life.

2. They do not allow democracy. They impose the Joochae ideology (totalitarian ideal) on people, with the aim of protecting and preserving the dictatorship's regime. They adhere to the

dictatorship and to a military-first policy. Any individuals who oppose this will be ruthlessly punished.

3. They deny private property.

4. They reject a free-market economy and employ a control-plan economy. They isolate themselves from the outside world.

5. They establish economic theories based on dissatisfaction, resentment, and hatred for personal wealth and prosperity. They insist on unreasonable equality in economic structure for hegemony and control, and flatly unfair equality in the distribution of profits and earnings. They reject free competition, which is the basis of a free-market economy.

6. There is no freedom of expression or freedom of the press. Individual opinions cannot be reflected in national policies. A sole Communist Party consisting of the small group of people with political power dominates the society, essentially like a dictatorship.

7. They suppress religions and believe in materialism. They are constructing a society governed by atheists.

8. North Korea implements lawless activities in domestic and foreign policy and implements diplomatic policies for the ultimate purpose of imposing its totalitarian, communist regime throughout the Korean peninsula and creating a communist empire.

9. North Korea demands the withdrawal of U.S. forces from South Korea and the abandonment of the alliance between the Republic of Korea and the United States. North Korea declared that the above two conditions are the prerequisite steps to the unification of the Korean peninsula. Their hidden intention of these demands is clearly the purpose described in the preceding issue (8). In order to obtain funds needed for maintaining the

dictatorship's regime, North Korea would dare to take any necessary means, including military action.

10. The ROK government ought to establish policies that magnanimously forgive any individuals or organizations that repent of their past mistakes or wrongdoings done from their ignorance and greed, make proper compensation with a true apology, and come back to the free, democratic nation of the Republic of Korea.

11. Pray to God that freedom and democracy, economic prosperity accomplished by the cooperation of management and labor, and peaceful policies of the Republic of Korea may save North Korea, and that a truly free, democratic, united Korean nation may be born in our Korean peninsula after enduring the current pangs of birth.

God bless our country of the Korean people. When a free, democratic, united, republic of Korea is born in the Korean peninsula, I believe that it will pay tribute and express our thanks to those who died in the Korean War.

# PART TWO

## Math and Thoughts on Selfhood

# — Chapter 4 —

# My Hobby, Math, and
# Thoughts on Consciousness and Selfhood

## My Hobby, Math

One of my hobbies throughout my life has been to solve math problems. I enjoyed solving arithmetic problems in elementary school, and problems of algebra, geometry, probability, differential, calculus, and so forth in middle school through college. The more difficult a problem was, the more challenging and interesting was the problem solving whenever free time was available.

After my graduation from Seoul Medical College in 1947, I continued to pursue my math hobby. I attended math seminars once a week with colleagues who loved the study of math.

I participated in the weekly math seminar of the Department of Physiology at Seoul Women's Medical College together with chairman and professor Dr. Bong Han Kim and my senior and instructor, Dr. Kwang Soo Yun. At that time I was a teaching assistant in physiology. We studied and discussed Fourier's function.

In 1958, I became chairman of the Department of Physiology at Catholic Medical College in Seoul. I met Dr. Yun, the chemistry professor of the Catholic Medical Preparatory School in Seoul at our weekly seminar of physical chemistry during a summer vacation. We tried to solve problems at the end of each chapter in our text, *The Physical Chemistry*, by Walter I. Moore.

Physical chemistry problems concerned the motion of molecules, atoms, and particles; energy; temperature; changes in states of matter; etc. These problems were solved by the application of differential calculus.

When I tried to solve math problems, I concentrated, forgetting the outside world.

## My Search for a Mathematical Model Applicable to Biological Phenomena

I served as a surgeon in the Republic of Korea Air Force from 1953 to 1958, during the Korean War and after the truce. I was assigned to the Aeromedical Institute because my major was physiology in the doctoral course at Seoul National University Graduate School.

I had the opportunity to do research in aviation medicine. I read books and journals published by the United States Air Force, and some other literature in aviation medicine.

Pilots are often exposed to acceleration (g-force) during their flight. They can perform safe flights by tolerating the effects of g-force on the human body.

Although human tolerance against g-force was illustrated in graphs, there seemed to be no mathematical formulas that might express human tolerance depending on the magnitude of acceleration and the duration of exposure to it in flight. I began to feel a special interest in this problem. I made up my mind to carry out animal experiments in order to clarify a general mathematical formula that expresses the human tolerance to g-force.

I started experiments for my new research project. There were quite a few difficulties in performing experiments during the Korean War. I received valuable advice and guidance from the chief of the Aeromedical Institute, Col. Jae Wee Choi, MD.

I directly observed experimental results in which the rate of bodily response and survival in mice varied depending on the magnitude of g-force and the duration of exposure.

I was eventually successful in establishing a general formula expressing a functional relationship between the intensity of g-force and the duration of exposure and survival probability in mice.

I presented a paper about this research on November 29, 1956, at the Fifth Semi-Annual Medical Conference of the U.S. Far East Air Force, at Baguio, Philippines, chaired by Col. John P. Stapp, USAF (MC). After the conference, Col. Stapp and Major General Niese, who was the surgeon general of the U.S. Far East Air Force, flew to visit our aeromedical laboratory in Seoul. The paper was published in the *Journal of Applied Physiology* in the United States in 1959 [17]. This paper was the major subject of my doctoral dissertation.

I was discharged to the Republic of Korea Air Force Reserve in August 1958. After discharge, I was appointed the chairman of the Department of Physiology at the Catholic Medical College in Seoul. I dedicated myself to medical student education and research.

My Air Force research on g-force on mice provided momentum for further comprehensive experimental investigation to find a general formula that would express a mathematical relationship between the intensity of stimulus or insult and duration and the response in animals in various biomedical phenomena.

A great many results were obtained in research by the tremendous efforts of my investigators at the Department of Physiology. I summarized the research results in a paper that was published in the Republic of Korea *Journal of the National Academy of Sciences* in 1960 [18].

I'd like to express my deepest thanks to the late Dr. Chong Yun Lee, who was a professor of physiology at the Seoul National University College of Medicine, a member of the National Academy of Sciences, and the chairman of the Korean Physiological Society, for his valuable advice and recommendations, which made possible the publication of my article in the journal.

The original and ultimate purpose of my study was to find a general mathematical model that would actually calculate the probability of safe survival in humans and other living organisms exposed to any harmful or adverse circumstances, overcoming the risk.

I earnestly longed to find a natural law that might protect humans and other living organisms from dangers and diseases to which they were exposed. In this way, I wished to medically contribute to their lives and well-being. My ceaseless, sincere wish has been a constant motivating and driving force in my research throughout my life.

I came to America in June 1962. I wanted to apply the formula I had constructed in Korea to clinical fields and to further develop the formula as a general model.

I studied computer science for the first time in 1962. I learned how to use a personal computer in mathematics. It was amazing to see how fast and easily the computer performed very complicated math calculations. Computer-assisted calculation rendered me great assistance in my research in the United States.

I applied the general formula constructed in Korea to some research data published in American clinical and basic medical science journals that I had selected to study. I was able to find the applicability of my model formula. Research papers on these subjects were published in some American and international scientific journals in 1986 [19] and later [20].

## Calculus and Computers

I entered the University of Tennessee Graduate School in Memphis in 1962. I took a doctoral course in physiology.

For six months, I attended lectures given by Dr. C. W. Sheppard, who was a professor of physiology and the chief of the Computer Medical Institute at the University of Tennessee. Dr. George A. Sacher of Argonne National Laboratory (operated by the University of Chicago) wrote me a letter on August 29, 1962, informing me that Dr. Sheppard was one of the outstanding mathematical biologists in the United States.

I made a lot of effort to learn computer science, especially programming, for the first time in my life. At that time, computers used vacuum tubes before transistors were developed. Large computers were installed in the Computer Medical Institute building. Equipment for punch cards that used the FORTRAN language was placed beside the computers.

I took a final exam in the computer course in December 1962 at the end of six months. Dr. Sheppard gave me his advice. "Dr. Chung, what do you think about designing a new computer program for the research you did in Korea and letting our university computer execute your program that includes a mathematical calculation? This project could be a final exam for you in this computer course."

He added, "You would design a program in the FORTRAN language and enter your actual data. I feel that this project would be the most appropriate exam problem for you. What do you think of my suggestion?"

After I thought about his suggestion for a while, I agreed with Dr. Sheppard, because his suggested project seemed to me quite appropriate for my exam problem in the computer course. So I replied, "Thank you, Dr. Sheppard. I totally agree with your opinion. I'll try it and do my best to solve the problem as my assigned exam in the computer course."

Prof. Sheppard continued to give me a valuable and helpful advice and suggestions.

### Argonne National Laboratory

OPERATED BY THE UNIVERSITY OF CHICAGO
9700 SOUTH CASS AVENUE
ARGONNE, ILLINOIS

TELEGRAM WUX LB ARGONNE, ILL.        CLEARWATER 7-7711        TELETYPE TWX ARGONNE, ILL. 1710

August 29, 1962

AIRMAIL

Dr. Sung Jang Chung
The University of Tennessee
Department of Physiology
Memphis 3, Tennessee

Dear Doctor Chung:

Thank you for your letter of 9 and 28 July. I am very pleased to learn that you are now in this country to do graduate work in physiology. I have followed your work with great interest since I first became acquainted with it several years ago, and I am sure that the work you do at the University of Tennessee will be of great value to you. Dr. Sheppard is one of the outstanding mathematical biologists in the country and you are fortunate to have an opportunity to work with him.

It is my hope also that you will be able to visit Argonne while you are in this country. I wish you the greatest success in your work, and I look forward to meeting you in person.

Sincerely yours,

George A. Sacher
Division of Biological
and Medical Research

GAS:mab

## Letter from Dr. George A. Sacher

He said, "Dr. Chung, there is a problem you must solve. The problem is that the current computer can not perform calculus. The mathematical formula included in your article contains a calculus formula, doesn't it? If you are able to find a formula of approximation for the calculus, the computer may help you with fast and efficient calculation. When a formula of approximation is successfully discovered or developed, the problem of your project can be solved, applying it to your data on your animal experiments." He went on to say, "There is a recent publication named *Approximation for Digital Computers*. You may borrow the book at the university library and study it. If you discover a formula of approximation for your calculus equation, you may solve your exam problem. I hope you will make an effort."

I was stunned to hear Dr. Sheppard say that the computer that had been astonishingly developing could not perform calculus. It was hard for me to believe. It seems to me now that the reason why the computer was unable to carry out calculus is that the computer was based on a binary system and that, in contrast, calculus is based on the handling of infinitely minimal quantity in numbers.

I went to the university library and borrowed *Approximation for Digital Computers,* written by C. Hastings, Jr. [38]. I studied the book with great interest and enthusiasm.

Numerous mathematical formulas were contained in the book. I selected some of those formulas and applied them, with necessary modifications, to my mathematical formula, examining their applicability. It took me several days to derive a formula of approximation for calculus that might be applicable to my research data. It was all trial and error. But the first ray of hope for a formula that seemed applicable finally flashed after my tireless hard work. I decided to employ the formula of approximation that I had derived in my mathematical search.

I could consequently compile in FORTRAN and design a computer program for my research data in which the formula of approximation was used instead of the formula of the Gaussian normal frequency curve in my article.

I went to the Computer Medical Institute and made punch cards for my designed program. I put the punch cards into the huge computer and operated it for the first time in order to have the computer execute the program and print out the results.

I was really astonished and amazed to see that the computer executed my program and printed out the numerical results of calculation in less than two minutes. I remembered that it took me about one day to perform a manual calculation of the mathematical equations of integral calculus when I was in Korea.

I looked at the computer printout that showed strikingly instantaneous calculations. I compared the computer-assisted numerical results on survival probabilities in mice with those in my original article published in the *Republic of Korea Journal of the National Academy of Sciences* in 1960 [16].

At the moment when I confirmed a literally complete agreement between both sets of data on survival probabilities, manually calculated and computer derived from a mathematical predictive formula, I was overwhelmed with joy and wonder.

I submitted this computer printout as my exam paper to Dr. Sheppard on December 17, 1962. He was very pleased to have my exam paper. After his review of the printout, he gave me a score of 95 out of 100 and an E for excellence. He returned the exam paper to me a few days later.

If I had not received Dr. Sheppard's outstanding guidance, surely I would not have been able to develop and expand my research in the United States as I had hoped.

In 1986, twenty-four years after the computer exam paper had been returned to me, I could publish a paper that described the computer program in my exam paper and the pertinent research data that had been published in Korea in 1960. I introduced my mathematical model of "probacent"-probability equation applicable to biomedical phenomena for the first time to the academic world.

If the computer program with use of the formula of approximation for calculus was employed in biological research in which the Gaussian normal curve was applicable, the distribution of probability values would be quickly and easily calculated without referring to the table of Gaussian normal distribution that is included in most statistics books.

If a formula of approximation for the integral other than the normal frequency distribution could be found and employed, the computer would be able to calculate approximate probabilities of distribution.

One day after coming to America, on November 20, 1962, I presented Korean research on the effects of a drug, Metrazol, on mice to a seminar held in the Department of Physiology at the University of Tennessee in Memphis. Professors of basic medical departments were invited to the seminar.

After the seminar, reprints of my article in the *Journal of the National Academy of Sciences* were given to some of the professors who attended the seminar with my compliments. But there seemed to be no formal responses of agreement or disagreement in regard to my research. I felt kind of disappointed.

I was reading literature related to my new research on thyroid metabolism in my quiet research room of the Department of Physiology on December 22, 1962, during winter vacation. Dr. Sheppard unexpectedly visited me. I greeted him with much pleasure.

Prof. Sheppard said, "Dr. Chung, I have carefully and thoroughly read your reprint of the research done in Korea, spending many hours.

It took me seven hours to read and understand your summarized research that included the paper presented to our recent seminar in this department. I agree with the research results in your article."

$$Q = \frac{10}{\sqrt{2\pi}} \int_{-\infty}^{P} e^{-\frac{(P-50)^2}{200}} \, dp \quad \text{------------} \quad (1a)$$

$$P = 100 \left[ \log D - \log \left(0.1 + 2.61/t^{1.955}\right) \right] / \left[ \log \left(55 + 173.11/t^{1.955}\right) - \log \left(0.1 + 2.61/t^{1.955}\right) \right]$$

$Q$ = predicted mortality (%)
$D$ = dose of metrazol (mg/10g).
$t$ : time after administration (min.) $\quad\quad\quad (1b)$

The following equation of approximation for digital computers was used.

(Reference : Cecil Hastings, Approximations for Digital Computers. P.185  1955.

Function : $\Phi(x) = \frac{2}{\sqrt{\pi}} \int_{-\infty}^{x} e^{-t^2} dt \quad$ --- Range : $0 \leq x < \infty$

$$\Phi(x) = 1 - \frac{1}{(1 + a_1 x + a_2 x^2 + a_3 x^3 + a_4 x^4)^4} \quad \text{-----} (2)$$

$a_1 = .278393$     $a_3 = .000972$
$a_2 = .230389$     $a_4 = .078108$

Transformation :

$$t = \frac{(P-50)}{\sqrt{200}}, \quad dt = \frac{dP}{\sqrt{200}}, \quad X = \frac{(P-50)}{\sqrt{200}} \quad \text{-----}(3)$$

Integral · from $-\infty$ to $P$ :

if $P - 50 < 0$ --- $= 50\Phi(\infty) - 50\Phi\left(\frac{50-P}{\sqrt{200}}\right)$

$Q = 50 / (1 + a_1 x + a_2 x^2 + a_3 x^3 + a_4 x^4)^4 \quad \text{----} (4)$

if $P - 50 \geq 0$ --- $= 50\Phi(\infty) + 50\Phi\left(\frac{P-50}{\sqrt{200}}\right)$

$Q = 100 - 50 / (1 + a_1 x + a_2 x^2 + a_3 x^3 + a_4 x^4)^4 \quad \text{---} (5)$

(3) (4) (5) equations are used in my project.

Exam paper from computer programming course

FORTRAN statement paper

Computer printout results (portion of exam paper)

I was so glad to hear his kind and unexpected comment on my research done in my mother country, Korea. He continued, "I think that you would be better off to apply for a research grant to the United States Atomic Energy Commission, specifically for animal experiments on effects of radiation. I'd like to advise you to continue your own original research in America."

When I received formal recognition of my research work from Dr. Sheppard, who was highly knowledgeable and renowned as a mathematical biologist, I felt boundless joy. I have been grateful since, from the bottom of my heart, to Dr. Sheppard for his kind and valuable guidance and his recognition of my study after review of my paper, as well as his advice and encouraging me to continue my research work in the United States.

## A Difficult Mathematical Problem Solved in my Dream

After graduation from the Seoul National University College of Medicine, I entered the Seoul National University Graduate School and majored in physiology. At the same time I got a job as a teaching assistant at the Department of Physiology at Seoul Women's Medical College. I diligently studied physiology and worked hard faithfully to carry out my duty as a teaching assistant.

One of my medical college classmates, Shin Kyun Hwang, got a job as a teaching assistant at the Department of Physiology at Ewha Women's Medical College and majored in physiology after graduation from our medical college.

Two of us met for a math seminar at the Department of Physiology of the Seoul College of Medicine on Saturday afternoons. We studied calculus, covering one chapter of a textbook each week. We tried to solve exercises at the end of each chapter. We discussed and solved the problems with questions and answers when we met on Saturday. It was an enjoyable math seminar. After studying math for about one hour, we used to play a violin duet with pleasure.

We were exhilarated as we solved exercises and advanced every week. If we encountered a hard problem to solve, the unsolved problem was left as homework. Each of us was supposed to try solving it for the following week's seminar. A majority of difficult problems were solved at the subsequent seminar.

One time we encountered an extraordinarily hard problem that was repeatedly postponed as homework for several weeks. I continuously attempted to solve the same problem whenever I had free time. I concentrated and worked hard on mathematical reasoning.

One night I dreamed about a math problem. To my surprise, I got a solution of the problem in my dream. I was overwhelmed with joy to see that the problem was perfectly solved. I woke up at the moment of feeling joy in the dream.

I immediately looked for a pencil and paper. I wrote down the math calculation exactly as I had seen it in my dream, before I might forget it. A complete solution came out at the end of my writing. I felt so great. My joy was beyond expression. I shouted for joy, "Bravo!"

The next Saturday, I went to our math seminar and wrote up the solution of our unsolved problem on the blackboard. Hwang was astonished to see it and said, "How did you solve this hard problem? I'm really surprised."

I answered, "Well, an unbelievable thing has happened to me. I tried so hard to solve this problem for about one month, but I was not successful. One night this week, I dreamed about this problem and tried to solve it. It was unexpectedly solved in the dream. I was so happy. Then at this moment I woke up. As soon as I woke up, I wrote it down in a sheet of paper. It is exactly the same as what I have just written on the blackboard." I could not veil my excitement and joy when I told my story to Hwang.

I presume that when we encounter a difficult problem in this life and strongly and unceasingly think of it in order to solve it, it is transferred to our subconscious, which continues to think, reason, and find its solution.

I would like to believe that this invisible, subtle mental process is true, since I experienced the extraordinary phenomenon of the solution to a difficult math problem in my dream. I think that our conscious and subconscious minds are connected and work together in concert.

Hwang went to North Korea in 1950 prior to the outbreak of the Korean War. He became a major of the North Korean army during the war. My memory of our math seminar is still unforgettable after more than half a century.

One time I encountered another hard mathematical problem that was not solved in a dream but which I believe was probably solved in my subconscious. I had been thinking about a math problem for several months to find its solution. It was a hard differential calculus problem from my research aimed at finding a general mathematical formula that would express a relationship between intensity of stimulus, duration of exposure, and occurrence of response in organisms in biological phenomena.

One day I went to a health spa with my family in Atlanta, Georgia. After parking our car in a parking lot, we walked in a yard decorated with a beautiful flower garden. I enjoyed the beauty of the garden while walking.

At that moment, the math problem suddenly crossed my mind. I tried to solve it in my mind while walking. I instantly got an idea for its solution, like a flash in my mind. I hurried to the lobby of the health spa, where I got a pencil and paper and wrote down the calculation I had done mentally a moment before. The difficult-looking problem was clearly and correctly solved! This experience has been living in my memory. It seems to me that my subconscious continued to reason and perfectly solved the problem and then suddenly transferred the solution to my conscious mind. I published the solution of the math problem in an international computer journal, the *International Journal of Biomedical Computing,* in 1995 [21].

In 2004, S. C. Mehta and H. C. Joshi [51] of the Institute of Research for Medical Statistics, New Delhi, India, published their research article on an input for radiation risk evaluation in the Indian context of a population of 1.1 billion. They successfully applied my mathematical model, just as I had applied it to my research on life tables of the U.S. adult population in 1995 [21].

In 2007, I published an article entitled "Computer-assisted predictive formulas expressing survival probability and life expectancy in U.S. adults, men and women, 2001" [24]. A reviewer of my article wrote a comment to the editor of the journal, *Computer Methods and Programs in Biomedicine,* and said, "This is a relatively straightforward application of a survival probability equation developed by the author to a new set of actuarial data from the U.S. National Center for Health Statistics. The equation has been used in several articles, both by the author and by other researchers internationally. As such, it has proven its practical usefulness."

The mathematical model of the "probacent"-probability equation was developed in my five decades of search for a mathematical truth hidden in biomedical phenomena. It seems to me applicable as a general approximation method to make useful predictions of probable outcomes in a variety of biomedical phenomena.

## Thoughts about Consciousness and Self

I like to think about myself and the universe surrounding me, consciousness and mind, and matter in the physical world.

Matter can be measured with measuring equipment and is objective existence. Matter and consciousness coexist in this world. Material phenomena are in the objective world and objects of scientific investigation. Consciousness of self is in the subjective world and outside of scientific research with measuring devices (His Holiness the Dalai Lama, *The Universe in a Single Atom* [25]).

We human beings are composed of the body, made of material matter, and the conscious mind. I would like to analyze our consciousness.

I will call our consciousness, when we are awake, the waking consciousness or the manifest consciousness (ego consciousness). Our manifest consciousness is inactive and disappears during our sleep state as well as in general anesthesia, cerebral concussion, and coma. The consciousness that we feel in our dream state I will call the dreaming consciousness or the subconscious. The subconscious stores our memories. In neuroscience, memory is believed to be stored in the brain.

At this point I want to think deeply about my aforementioned special dream. The fact that my subconscious astonishingly solved a difficult math problem that my manifest consciousness was unsuccessful to solve for a long time, presents me with a great philosophical research subject.

The master actor who acted in the mathematical reasoning in my manifest consciousness was a personality of "I." Then who was the personality that performed math calculations in reasoning and found the solution in my dream state? Although it was felt as "I" in the dream, it seems to me logical that there was another personality in the subconscious activity. My self feels and thinks in my ordinary life, and another personality in my selfhood acts in the dream. Therefore, two personalities seem to exist together in my consciousness and subjectively compose my self.

Our manifest consciousness is deeply related to our bodily functions and associated with the brain. It recognizes the surrounding environment through the five senses, bodily response to and manipulation of the outer world, thinking, and so forth. I name this personality the "physical self." The physical self may be called as the "little self." The person who represents the little self is also called the "little man" in Confucianism.

The master of the subconscious, who acts in the deeper portion of the self, can be called the "inner self." The inner self may also be called the "big self." The person who represents the big self is called the "great man" in Confucianism. Consequently, it seems to me that my self is living as two personalities, the physical and the inner self.

According to teachings of ancient sages, the inner self is endowed with extraordinary reasoning, great wisdom, broad knowledge, clairvoyance, precognition, telepathy, and creative power. The inner self also keeps our memory.

When man is born to this planet, Earth, the connection between the physical and the inner self appears to be blocked and checked by a screen of inconceivable, unknown mechanisms. So we apparently feel only our physical selves as our selves during most of our waking hours. We do not primarily feel our inner selves. But we know that the inner self controls the physical self that is confined within the physical body; it does this by means of conscience, intelligence, responses to beauty and art, justice, noble will, morality, and creative power.

Our memory is stored in groups of brain cells via nervous connections, physicochemical processes in nerves and the brain. It seems to me that at the same time, the memory seems to be transmitted to and stored in the subconscious—the inner self.

Dreams arise as the outermost activity of the inner self when the waking consciousness, or the manifest consciousness, enters an inactive state and disappears. The dreaming consciousness belongs to the subconscious. The waking consciousness and the dreaming consciousness appear to be close to each other. Here, I infer that the physical consciousness associated with the brain and the subconscious of the inner self interact and permeate one another, mutually feeling each other and arising in the mind of the self. Usual, ordinary dreams are thought to be memory activities produced by the brain in the subconscious and belonging to activities of the physical self. In contrast, a special dream of precognition, intelligence, or unbelievable mathematical calculation for solving a hard math problem is believed to be the conscious mind of the inner self.

Feelings of eating, drinking, running, etc. in the waking consciousness are accompanied by actual physical actions; those feelings in the dreaming consciousness are, however, not accompanied by physical actions, and merely indicate psychological phenomena.

The inner self is the real "I" of the subconscious and considered to be like the structure of an object. The physical self is consciously felt as the seemingly real "I," but the physical self as well as the physical consciousness (the waking consciousness) also disappears. The physical self, the apparent "I," is a misunderstood illusion that is the root of human ignorance and suffering. The inner self is always existing and indestructible. There will be no physical self without the physical body. We might think this way: the physical self is like a bubble that arises from water and disappears in it. The ego of our daylight hours rises up from the subconscious of the self, just like a bubble or a wave from a sea. We are not aware of this phase transfer.

The physical self and the inner self are thought to be inconceivably connected and interact as the manifest consciousness and the subconscious are connected in the memory process, constituting our selfhood.

If thoughts, words, and emotions are intense and persistent, they are transmitted to and impressed upon the inner self in our deeper portion. For example, my inner self correctly and clearly solved my difficult math problem. Difficult problems in arenas of science, technology, economy, politics, music, art, and literature may be likewise successfully solved by our inner selves when we make sincere and unceasingly prolonged efforts for a long time.

We cannot conclude the nonexistence of anything merely because it cannot be seen. The fact that science has not yet proved the existence of God does not indicate that God does not exist. We cannot conclude that the inner self does not exist solely because we cannot see it. We must avoid dogmatism in science (His Holiness the Dalai Lama [25]).

The physical world is of four dimensions and objects of scientific research. In contrast, the physical self and the inner self are not clear in terms of dimension and outside scientific investigations.

What is the essential body of the self? According to teachings of sages, the essence of self is arcane and of no birth and of no death, immortal and indestructible, eternal soul.

My conclusion, based on lifelong philosophical contemplation and reasoning about my experiences related to my math hobby and my special dream, is as follows: *The human self is an individual identity in whom the physical self (little self) and the inner self (big self) coexist as one.*

# PART THREE

## Thoughts on Self, Universe, and Life

# — CHAPTER 5 —

## My Thoughts on the Universe and the Self, Matter and Mind, and the Self in Consciousness

I would like to think of all sentient beings that live together with human beings on the Earth; also upon the nature of the boundless universe. It seems to me that consciousness may pervade animals, trees, flowers, rocks, mountains, seas, earth, sun, moon, and stars; that is, each constituent of nature. Isn't it true? We cannot feel another person's consciousness. We likewise cannot feel consciousness inside objects of nature. We cannot conclude that consciousness does not exist in matter, because science cannot prove it (His Holiness the Dalai Lama [25]).

I would like to contemplate about matter on the basis of quantum theories in modern physics (John Gribbin, *Quantum Physics* [35]; Stephen Hawking, *A Brief History of Time* [41]). When we enter the subatomic microscopic fields, electrons behave as particles as well as waves—in dual forms at the same time. The essential form of particles and waves is energy that is an ability to work with power in space. They are not solid, tangible substances. Energy is action or a process of action without solid substance; that is, matter. Action of energy without solid substance manifests as matter in space. This is the true phase of matter in empty space as discovered by quantum mechanics.

The relationship between energy *(E)* and mass *(m)* can be represented by the following famous equation of Einstein's:

$E = mc^2$ ( $c$ = the speed of light )

According to theories experimentally proven by quantum mechanics, emergence and disappearance of particles that carry mass *(m)* occur in space. Empty space abundantly contains hidden, fundamental, virtual particle-antiparticle pairs of matter such as electron-positron pairs, proton-antiproton pairs, and neutron-antineutron pairs (Fritjof Capra, *The Tao of Physics* [14]). The term "virtual" means being empty in a physical sense; that is, invisible, intangible, and immeasurable by scientific methods.

If external energy comes to a region of space, it will be excited, fluctuate, pulsate and then make a hidden, virtual particle-antiparticle pair emerge in it, causing material actualization, or creation of matter (George Henning, *Nothingness* [32]).

In contrast, when a particle of positive energy and an antiparticle of negative energy collide and unite in space, they are annihilated and form a hidden, virtual particle-antiparticle pair and disappear out of existence (annihilation of matter), simultaneously releasing a photon in the space (Fritjof Capra [14]). A photon is a light wave and its own antiparticle. Subatomic particles are also mutually transformable according to quantum theories. Energy is the essential phase of the physical world. All things are vibrating energy with duality of particle and wave of various frequencies and shapes. Empty space, a vacuum, is not nothingness in the sense of physical reality. Emergence and disappearance of matter, as forms of energy, in empty space are the inherent nature of space, the vacuum, the void. Empty space can be recognized as the mother of matter and thus of all things. The void of cosmic space has the potential of infinite creative energy.

I would like to infer that when a matter-antimatter pair collides, disintegrates, and disappears in space, then at the same time, consciousness in each half of the pair, electron, atom, and molecule would disappear. Empty space contains hidden virtual consciousness. If a mental-force stimulus of mental energy strikes the space, then the space could manifest consciousness. Consciousness emerges and disappears in empty space like a water bubble or a wave that arises and disappears in a vast ocean. Consciousness (mind) and matter are interconnected, interrelated, and interdependent (Fritjof Capra, *The Tao of Physics* [14]). When matter disappears, it is most likely that consciousness simultaneously disappears, and vice versa. When matter emerges, consciousness also seems to emerge, and vice versa.

All things of the universe have dual aspects: material and mental aspects, as an electron with a duality of particle and wave. Self recognizes subatomic particles by its built-in consciousness of wave form. Self also recognizes subatomic particles by measurement with scientific equipment or observing their material aspects.

All things—electrons, atoms, molecules, rocks, cells, plants, flowers, trees, mountains, the Earth, the sun, the moon, stars—appear to have dual aspects: one aspect of matter composed of physical energy, and another aspect of consciousness, of thought, feeling, emotion, instinct, intelligence, and possibly self-awareness of various degrees (George Applegate, *The Complete Book of Dowsing* [2]; William Buhlman, *Adventures Beyond the Body* [12]). The physical self ("I") in man is inherently formed of the body and the conscious mind.

In Confucianism, this empty space is named *Moogeuk* (无極), the Non-Ultimate (Wu Chi). *Moogeuk* bears all things. In Laozi's writings, it is said that the named Nothingness is the beginning of heaven and earth, and that the named Being is the mother of all things. These statements seem to me to similarly express the physical phenomena described above. Nothingness, empty space, the void, is the root from which heaven and earth begin, and when Nothingness becomes Being, it becomes the mother of all things—of the physical world, of matter.

It also seems to me that mental activities, thoughts and emotions of the inner self, can create electromagnetic-like, subtle, physical energy in the space, acting upon material elements of electromagnetic quality that appear to have consciousness, and then inducing changes in the material state. Mental energy springs up from the omnipresent creator god. In physics, four forces—gravitational force in the gravitational field, electromagnetic force in the electromagnetic field, and strong nuclear and weak nuclear force in the Higgs field—are recognized. A mental force in the consciousness field could be added as another force to these four forces in the universe.

Masaru Emoto wrote in his book *The Secret Life of Water* [29] that he has recently discovered amazing natural phenomena. Water can produce a variety of forms of snow crystals that are dependant on human thoughts and feelings.

Gratitude, enjoyment of beautiful music, and love in the conscious mind act on water molecules, producing snow crystals of beautiful shapes. Emoto proved it with photographs of those occurrences and published his findings to the world. What has been proven in the relationship between mind and matter is that our minds can create physical energy in space and that consciousness probably exists in the matter of water molecules.

The fundamental elements of matter—electrons, protons, photons, quarks, leptons, etc.—are particles composed of energy and simultaneously waves of certain frequencies and composed of energy, showing dual qualities. It seems to me that consciousness probably exists, inherently superposed upon the outer dual aspects of subtle particle and wave of each particle.

All things in the physical world vibrate with unique frequencies of energy in empty space, as David Hawkins [40] and Richard Gerber [33] wrote in their books. Each vibrating wave of all things is emitted, spreads out, and propagates in all directions into the universe and is received by all other things. The physical world and the world of consciousness coexist in the universe and interact with each other.

Consequently, as aforementioned, self, especially the inner self, is believed to be able to create energy and change matter, together with omnipotent God, who governs the whole universe. Can we not say that in this sense, man participates in creation with the creator, God? Buddha taught that all things in the universe are created by the power of thought (His Holiness the Dalai Lama, *How To See Yourself* [26]). According to Jesus's teachings, when we pray to God with deep faith, we can move a mountain from a place to another place (Matthew 17:20; 21:21–2). I feel that I might vaguely understand this teaching of Jesus. All power of the self comes from God.

When we have firm beliefs and thoughts at this present moment in our waking consciousness, they will be transferred to the inner self that is endowed with unimaginably enormous knowledge, the power of receiving information, and creative power. The inner self creates mental energy, affecting the material world and bringing material actualization. Beliefs cause reality. The point of action of mental power is the present moment.

As Adam wrote in his book *The Path of the Dream Healer* [1], quantum particles in DNA will react to and be influenced by light emitted from thoughts. It is inferable that thoughts create subtle, light energy waves and influence DNA molecules in cells like various-shaped snow crystals formed by different thoughts, as Emoto proved [29]. DNA may therefore react to thoughts, as Adam wrote.

At this point in my reasoning, we have to think how to avoid confusion, dogmatism, and ignorance. The process in which self creates matter composed of particles and waves is believed to be unidirectional. God creates all things in the universe in one direction. A reverse direction of this God-creative process does not exist. In other words, matter or physical bodies cannot create the self, or soul. Matter is the energy of created things. Matter of positive energy can be annihilated by antimatter of negative energy. God is the creator and the master of creative activities. The artist creates art products, but the art products cannot create an artist. As Buddha said, all things in the universe are illusion (maya) and emptiness, and names only, created by the mind.

I think more about the self according to teachings of sages of ancient and modern times of all ages, and of the East and the West. Buddha taught that there is Buddha nature in our selfhood. Thich Nhat Hanh wrote in his forward in the book *The Dhammapada,* translated by Ananda Maitreya [50], that there is a Buddha in each of us. Jesus taught that "Father is in me, and Father and I are one" ( John 10:30, 38; 14:10). Jae Woo Choi, the founder of a Korean religion, Chondokyo [16], declared that man is heaven. In Christianity, man is the son of God.

In other doctrines of sages, a third personality, the super self of Buddha nature or divinity, exists within ourselves. The self exists as an individual part of a whole self inconceivably composed of superposed plural personalities (Alice Bailey, *The Consciousness of the Atom* [7]). It seems to me that the plural personalities are composed of the physical, the inner, and the super selves. The super self is a part of God. Persons who are spiritually enlightened and have reached the state of the super self are called sages, buddhas, godly men, avatars, or gurus in all ages and in the East and the West.

The consciousness of the super self seems to exist in the deeper portion of the subconscious, in the super-consciousness of Self. Man has the potential of God with the super self.

When waking up, the manifest consciousness arises from the subconscious and faces toward the physical world. It senses, perceives, and reacts with the physical body, and it also interacts with and responds to the thoughts of the inner self. While sleeping, the waking or manifest consciousness disappears. During sleep, there will be only the subconscious part of the brain and the inner and super selves.

During the day, we feel that the master of the physical self appears to be the true "I," but this feeling seems to be an illusion and a misconception (His Holiness the Dalai Lama [26]). We humans are prone to fall in this pit of illusion and ignorance. Our senses contribute to this illusion. The physical self felt as the permanent "I" in the waking consciousness is the false self (non-self), as the impermanent physical body and the physical self will be left behind and disappear out of being at death, when the true self inhabiting the body leaves. The consciousness of the brain of the physical self can emerge and vanish like matter in the void. But the true self—the inner self and the super self—is eternal, the true soul, with no birth and no death. Man has dual selves: the transitory, false, physical self, and the true self of the inner and super self at the higher level. The physical self and the physical body belong to the created world. The true self of the inner/super self is part of God.

The spiritual world of the true self is inconceivably multiple, potentially infinite in dimension, and seems to be spaceless and timeless. The universal cosmic consciousness exists in everything in the universe. God is omnipresent in the infinitely vast space of the universe and in every infinitely microscopic region of space. God is transcendent and immanent. The universe is a manifestation of the cosmic consciousness, the body of God, the creator. God, the cosmic consciousness, dwells as the true self in man. God is named in religions as Heavenly Father, Jehovah, Buddha nature, Heaven, Tao, Allah, or Brahman.

The physical self appears to exist but does not exist, as taught by Buddhism. It has a phase of emergence and disappearance. Nothingness of self (the physical self) in Buddhist teachings, killing the body and achieving love in Confucianism's teachings, and the teaching of Christianity that whoever loses his life for Jesus will find eternal life (Matthew 10:39, 16:25)—all of these teachings clearly tell that the physical self is an illusion and that the inner self and the super self are the true self and eternal. The physical self is void and impermanent, as the physical body is non-self. The false "I" is like a reflected moon in water, like an image in a mirror or a holographic image that appears to be a real, solid object. As Buddha said, "Look. Spirits and human beings think their non-selves are their real selves and are attached to their names and forms, believing those false selves are their true selves." (Suppanipata, 756, 790).

David Hawkins wrote in his book *Power vs. Force* [40] that the human ego is actually not an "I" at all; this illusion of an apparently separate, individual "I" ego is the source of all human suffering. The above statements seem to me to imply that the individual "I" is connected all of the other ones, not a separate, illusory ego in the cosmic drama.

As the prophet Muhammad (570–632) taught in the Qur'an and the Hadith, he who knows his own self knows God. Learn to know yourself. The present world is only an illusory pleasure (3:185). God is both transcendent and immanent. The most excellent jihad is the conquest of one's own ego. There is no compulsion in religion (2:256). Every religion has a special character, and the character of Islam is modesty. According to Ziauddin Sardar, as written in his book *What*

*Do Muslims Believe?* [62], "jihad" means "striving": any earnest striving in the way of God, involving personal, financial, intellectual, or physical effort, for righteousness and against oppression or wrongdoing. Karen Armstrong wrote in her book *Islam* [3] that the Qur'an teaches that the only just war is a war of self-defense.

The true self is the union of the human-self of the inner self and the divine-self of the super self at the higher level, which is an eternal soul of no birth and no death. God dwells in our selves as the super self. But man does not know this and searches for God not within the self, but instead in the outside world. We are all one with part of God within us. Our separation from each other and from God is an illusion and a source of ignorance.

Historic facts written in the biography of Edgar Cayce, the "sleeping prophet" (1877–1945), provide some of the best evidence concerning the above-stated thought of the physical self and the inner self. Edgar Cayce, who had no medical education, made accurate diagnoses and gave effective prescriptions to thousands of patients from all over the world in his "physical readings" while asleep. The works performed by Cayce during his sleep were well-documented (Andrew O'Loughlin, *Famous Precognitive and Problem-Solving Dreams and Others* [55]). He heard questions and requests given to him by awake persons in his hypnotic trance sessions.

In Cayce's case, it can be inferred that Cayce's physical self disappeared while he was asleep, and that his real, inner self's consciousness began to act, seemingly to hear, think, and talk by using his body's sense organs. His inner self seemed to possess clairvoyance, enormous memory, and amazing medical knowledge. The true self—the inner and super self—of Edgar Cayce is believed to have done great works of Christlike compassion to help thousands of suffering patients for forty years.

The brain that controls all sense organs and visceral organs of the body appears to be activated by the physical self or the inner self in the waking and sleeping states. Further, the central nervous system, including the brain, may be activated by another spiritual entity if allowed by the inner self, as seen in mediumistic psychic phenomena. All things are possible with God (Matthew 10:20, 19:26).

Edgar Cayce unequivocally proved the wonderful truth that man has the clairvoyant faculty through his inner self when his physical self disappears during his sleep.

The super self seems to exist in the deeper portion of the subconscious. Man seems to have God-given potential. In Confucianism, it is said that God and man possess the same virtues.

The all-knowing and almighty creator God is present on the other side of the grand subconscious of the invisible cosmic consciousness existing behind visible nature. The cosmic consciousness keeps all events of the universe through space and time, and it retains human history as part of a universal memory of nature, called the "akashic record" in Indian philosophy, the counterpart of human memory kept in the human subconscious. According to Ervin Laszlo [45], the akashic record is the lasting record of all that has happened and will happen in the whole universe.

Man's self is part of God, like a water drop is part of the ocean, and lives on this side of human consciousness. The universe and man are of same essential quality and interconnected. We do not realize that we are with God. The grand subconscious or cosmic consciousness is like an ocean, and the little consciousness of man is like a bubble or a wave. Both are essentially the same water. The self (soul) is immortal, indestructible, and eternal, together with God, the universal soul. Our individual souls participate in God's creation as co-creators.

## — CHAPTER 6 —

## What Is the Purpose of Life?

We are born to this Earth. We have physical selves inside our bodies. The physical self is imprisoned in the body of flesh and bone. Our minds perceive the physical world through our senses and are restrained by desire, pleasure, ignorance, arrogance, selfishness, and uncontrollable ego, with the fixed idea of the false physical self as the true self.

The mind of the physical self wanders with worry, fear, and restlessness. But we know that we have consciences that can control our minds, which behave like fish being thrown out of water and flapping around, as Buddha said (The Dhammapada, 34 [54]). When we act and speak in compliance with our self-controlling consciences, we feel true joy. Conscience is the voice of the inner self. I use the terms "inner self," "true self," "super self," or "soul" with the same meaning: counterparts of the physical self.

The inner self existing in the deep portion of selfhood at a higher level makes efforts to live following and obeying the super self of divinity and Buddha nature in a deeper portion at a much higher level. The inner self is attracted toward the super self and is characterized by wisdom, love, compassion, humility, responsibility, faith, morality, courage, beauty, and creativity. The mind occupied by the inner self is peaceful, cheerful, and happy in compliance with the cosmic laws.

Free will is given by God to man (Gina Cerminara, *Many Mansions* [15]), to both the physical self and the inner self, allowing autonomy. Free will is carried out by the mind-occupying, false, physical self or the inner self. Human actions are done by conscious mind occupied by either the physical self or the inner self.

The physical self acts, following desire-oriented free will that is connected to the brain. Therefore, it is extremely important that the inner self controls the physical self every moment by positively occupying the conscious mind as the sanctuary of God, directing actions with free will, and truly performing God's will. As Buddha said, "One who conquers himself is the supreme conqueror, rather than those who fight in the battlefield and conquer a million enemies." I believe that the term "himself" here implies his own physical self as an enemy (The Dhammapada, 66, 103 [53]).

As the guru Yogananda said, "You are your own enemy, and you don't know it" *(Spiritual Diary* [75]). I believe that this means that your physical self is the enemy of your true self.

How do we discipline and control the physical self, which has an inherent tendency to think and act in order to seek desire and pleasure (David Bohm [54])? First of all, the conscious mind will be emptied and then there will be no thoughts and no ideas. The empty mind is the sanctuary for emergence of the true self. The voice of the inner self, conscience, will follow. As Yogananda said, "By constantly following the inner voice of conscience, which is the voice of God, you will become a truly moral person, a highly spiritual being, a man of peace" *(Spiritual Diary* [77]).

I feel that the following three things the sages have taught us are important: First, control the desire of the physical body, and then get rid of the mental illusion of the false physical self—ego ("I") appearing as the true self—in order to discipline the mind and act. This illusion is felt to be the hardest thing to conquer in this life.

Second, keep the Golden Rule: Do to others what you want others to do to yourself. Be kind, and forgive others. Be harsh and strict to yourself.

Third, do meditation and prayer. Devote yourself.

Suppose that the physical self—which is primarily ego-centered, concerned about and working for the outer physical world, following fleshly desires—commits a wrong thing. This action ("sowing") causes a reaction of the inner self to contemplate in order to compensate for the evil action ("reaping") in the inner self's consciousness. This is probably because the inner self is solely responsible for any actions done by the physical self under its supervision.

To me, this action/reaction in the self seems like the action/reaction in the macroscopic Newtonian physical world, and like matter and antimatter in the quantum world. The reaction of the inner and super self complies with the cosmic law, the karmic law (Fritjof Capra [16]), the law of cause and effect of the universe (Mark 4:24, Luke 6:37–8 ). "Whatsoever a man soweth, that shall he also reap" (Galatians 6:7).

It seems to me that the relationship between the physical self and the true self is analogous to driving a car. The driver is the true self, and the steering wheel and the engine are the physical self. The car is in a nearly automatic driving condition. The road is considerably narrow and winding. A high cliff is on one side of the road, and an ocean is on the other side, very close to the road. The driving situation in the physical world full of illusions (maya) and temptations is really treacherous and risky. The driver (true self) controls the steering wheel with reason, conscience, and willpower in guiding the car. The driver is constantly watching the car (operated by the physical self). The driver must be alert and careful, ready to slow down, turn, or stop the car at any moment if needed. The true self is also endeavoring to be calm and feel his total responsibility in driving. The physical self would not be blamed or charged for any wrong driving or accidents that might result in bodily injuries and automobile insurance problems. The above analogy might be comparable and understandable in view of the karmic law.

The true self carries out the reaction in the future. The true self reaps what the physical self sows. The soul of the true self will pay all karmic debts that mean victory against the physical self. It is necessary for the true self to grow and develop, and to achieve self-realization and enlightenment, endeavoring to unite with God. The karmic law is actually freely chosen by the true self, taking responsibilities and desiring to achieve higher goals of experience, education, and redemption (John Edward, *One Last Time* [27]).

It seems to me that according to karmic law, the sacrosanct free will of the inner self, the soul of the individual, is not infringed upon with forcing by others. As John Edward wrote, "We are not punished on the Other Side, except by ourselves" [29].

The planet Earth is a school of spiritual education and training for the soul and a ground of struggling actions between the false physical self and the true inner self for development and growth.

Jesus taught that we should love God with all our hearts, souls, and minds, and that we should love our neighbors as ourselves (Matthew 22:37-39). Buddha taught disciples to meditate, keep commandments, and perform devotions. He also taught love and compassion and the eight right paths: right view, right thought, right speech, right conduct, right living, right effort, right conception, and right concentration. These lead us to the great freedom (Jacky Sach, *The Everything Buddhism Book* [61]).

The supreme purpose of man in this life is a divine mission of self-realization to unite with God. By overcoming ignorance as the source of all suffering, with insight into the true nature of the self, we can prevent our narrow-minded and selfish egos of the false "I" (the physical self) from blocking us from reaching the endlessly high goal. As Lao Tzu said, "The Tao goes forever, doing nothing, yet everything gets done" (Tao Te Ching: 37; Fritjof Capra [14], [44]).

It seems to me that the true self is eternal, having the physical self do nothing; everything gets done by the true self. When we live facing toward and being united with our true selves, we presumably enter the level that Confucius referred to by saying, "At the age of seventy, I follow my desire and will not pass beyond the rules of morality." As Jesus said, "Be perfect, therefore, as your Heavenly Father is perfect" (Matthew 5:48). As Gautama said, Buddha is a perfect man (Suttanipata 481, 560 [53]).

We should overcome the physical self, realize the inner self, and devote ourselves to the spiritual growth of all of us, and carry out our duties and God's will.

In order to achieve the purpose of life, we engage in discipline of the mind, seek insight into the truth, meditate (yoga), pray, and render service to others, our brothers and sisters.

### Teachings in Islam

The prophet Muhammad taught in Islam, "Do you love your God? Love your fellow being first. No man is a true believer unless he desires for his brother what he desires for himself. Be good to your parents, to relatives, to orphans, to the needy, to neighbors near and far, to travelers in need, and to yourselves. Feed the hungry and visit the sick, free the captive if he is unjustly confined, and assist the oppressed. God does not change the condition of a people until they change their own condition (13:11). Islam does not condone frivolous pleasure, lying, slander, arrogance, boasting, scheming, obscenity, insult, spite, envy, or inconstancy. Do not monopolize. Give the laborer his wages before his perspiration dries. The trustful and trustworthy merchant is associated with prophets, martyrs, and the upright. The world is green and beautiful, and God has appointed you his stewards over it" (Ziauddin Sadar, *What Do Muslims Believe?* [62]).

## Leaders in Economic, Political, Educational, and Scientific fields

Leaders in economic and financial enterprises seek not only profits through fair competition in free markets with increased productivity and efficiency, better quality, and reduced price for consumers, but they also seek public benefits and cooperative, mutually supportive, and morality-based social contribution [57].

Marvelous discoveries of science and development of technology will hopefully bring unimaginable well-being to humanity (Michio Kaku, *Physics of the Impossible* [42]) and found a paradise on Earth.

When we focus our conscious minds on positive thoughts of love, compassion, faith, and gratitude, these thoughts and emotions will be transferred from our manifest consciousness to the subconscious, and then the inner self will carry out creative activities. Special waves of certain frequencies in the physical world will resonate with the energy-creating thought waves of the inner self.

We humans must believe in God's love, realize within ourselves the God-given marvelous, true self, and bear unyielding beliefs. We must not think about unhappy or ugly experiences of the past, and we must not anticipate disaster or failure in the future. At this present moment we must keep our firm beliefs, bright hopes, and joy, concentrate our full strength, and endeavor. We will utilize enormous gifted wisdom and knowledge and creative power of our true self. We will be able to successfully achieve our goals and ideals, because the creative potential of the true self springing out from God's creative energy of the universe is inconceivably great, together with God's boundless grace.

# — CHAPTER 7 —

## Special Thoughts on the Space
## in which Consciousness Occurs

On the basis of the above-described teachings of sages, scientific findings, and my logical reasoning, it seems to me true that the space of the universe that is perceived as a vast, empty, and boundless void, called Nothingness (无) in Taoism, *Moogeok* (无極, Wu Chi) in Confucianism, and the Emptiness (空) in Buddhism, is the place in which consciousness of mind and energy of matter constantly arise and disappear with no known beginning or ending.

Consciousness of mind seems to be an inconceivably subtle form of wave energy of ultrahigh frequency. Matter proves not to be a solid substance; instead it is merely vibrating energy in a form of low-frequency waves in space. Therefore, consciousness and energy appear to be vibrating products created in space.

The physical self (the ego) feels itself in its conscious mind. Conscious feelings and thoughts appear intimately associated with the physical body, ultimately with the brain (matter). The physical body and the physical self are products of creation, representing the phases of matter and consciousness of space like both sides of a coin.

The consciousness of the physical self and the matter of the physical body are part of the created world (maya) that constitutes darkness and ignorance because they do not know and cannot see their creator. They have no idea where they come from and where they are going after death. They are so tiny compared to the vast universe. Their mind is so limited. They can't see outside the visible range of frequencies of electromagnetic waves. They can't hear beyond the audible range of sound waves.

They feel they are living in the bright, wonderful world, but in reality they live in the darkness, being blind, deaf, and ignorant.

An infinite number of real and virtual waves of consciousness and energy of myriad different frequencies coexist in each region of space. This can be inferred from a well-known physical phenomenon in which countless real electromagnetic waves of different frequencies coexist in empty space. The mind feels and perceives selected waves of consciousness as a sensation or a thought, as a television set gets selected images and sounds in its screen, depending on tuning to their frequencies of electromagnetic waves in space.

Telepathy between two persons seems possible on the basis of real waves of consciousness existing in space. Precognition between a person and his environment might be achieved by tapping real and virtual waves of consciousness of the environment.

Whenever a region of space is stimulated and excited, stored virtual consciousness of memory might come into reality as memory in human consciousness. It seems possible in this way to tap into natural or human history or its evolving processes.

In space, a field of consciousness and energy can be occupied by the physical self or the inner/super self, the soul. The conscious mind in space can be abolished by medical anesthetics, by blocking out brain functions, and by an unknown brain-blocking mechanism during sleep.

In addition, the conscious mind can be made void by meditation of the inner self in which the conscious mind can be silent, without thought, serene, peaceful, and blissful. When the conscious mind is crystal clear, the light of the creator, God, enters the sanctuary of the self.

In order to keep the conscious mind clear, pure, and void, it seems imperatively important not to see ugly, impure things, not to hear immoral things, and not to think ignorant or self-centered thoughts.

The ego has no sense of responsibility or ethical principles for its actions, which are primarily aimed at seeking desire and pleasure (Lee Nichol, *The Essential David Bohm* [54]). The physical self is basically insane and so cannot be condemned for its selfish, robot-like activities.

The true self seems to be able to simultaneously feel or think of the same conscious, subtle waves caused by the physical self, the ego. The true self monitors and supervises all happenings in the field of consciousness caused by the physical self. This space is a common working place for both the physical self and the inner self.

The true self is the soul; that is, the inner self endowed with the super self of potential divinity. The soul acts in compliance with God's laws, makes efforts with unyielding faith to achieve self-realization, suppressing the physical self's selfish and ignorant behavior, and then enters a silent, serene sanctuary of the self, the creator God.

The true self is part of the creator, who is the indestructible and unknowable substance of eternal existence. As Jesus said, man is created in the image of God. The true self works with God. He makes efforts to please God. He is happy and cheerful in pleasing him.

The true self, the soul, is a spark of the creator, God. The light of this spark illuminates and abolishes the darkness and the ignorance of the physical self, the ego. At the same time, it seems to cleanse the body cells with good and beautiful feelings and wisdom that probably reconstructs each cell with the creation of beautiful molecular crystals within the cell, as pretty snow crystals are formed from water by beautiful thoughts (Masaru Emoto, *The Secret Life of Water* [30]). Then the cleansed body will obey the true self's dictates, behave in compliance with God's laws, and glorify God.

Considering physicist David Bohm's theory [10] (Lee Nichols, *The Essential David Bohm* [54]) that a space of one cubic centimeter stores an unimaginably huge amount of energy, it is also imaginable and believable that each region of the space is filled with the boundless love of the creator, God. He gives sunshine and rain to all of us, good or bad, as Jesus said. The mysterious and wonderful but unknowable space appears empty but seems to be filled with God's love for both of the physical self and the true self as well as all other creatures. The space is also believed to be filled with God's limitless knowledge, wisdom, and bliss. We children of the creator need to empty our minds and open them to our Heavenly Father. As Jesus said, "So I say to you: Ask, and it will be given to you; seek, and you will find; knock, and the door will be opened to you. For everyone who seeks receives, he who seeks and finds; and to him who knocks, the door will be opened" [Luke 11:10, 11]. The inner self will knock the door of the immanent super self by meditation (禪 定) and open the spiritual window to God, endeavoring to merge with the manifesting super self of potential divinity.

Ceaseless efforts (精 進) of the inner self to observe commandments and to perform meditation will gradually lead the soul to a higher state of manifestation of potential divinity on the road to self-realization, and to a higher degree of union with all-knowing and almighty God.

A son of God who achieves full divinity becomes an enlightened man, like Jesus, Gautama, and Maitreya. He and God are one and perfect.

Silent, invisible, intangible, empty space, or nothingness, seems to be our Father's unknowable substance of eternal, indestructible existence with no beginning and with no ending.

I humbly pray that the above-written statements are true.

July 2, 2007

# PART FOUR

## New Quantum Theories and Modern Science

# — CHAPTER 8 —

## New Quantum Theories in Modern
## Physics Proposed by David Bohm

Modern physicists researching quantum mechanics discovered three unexpected and inexplicable findings that required extraordinary new speculation and efforts to explain (Lee Nichol, *The Essential David Bohm* [54]). Dr. David Bohm, a well-known physicist (1917–92) proposed new quantum theories (*Wholeness and the Implicate Order* [10]) to explain the three new phenomena using his outstanding scientific and philosophical reasoning and imagination. Science and religion come so close now to each other in their world views, taking into account David Bohm's quantum theories (Michael Talbot, *The Holographic Universe* [66]).

Matter *(e.g.,* electrons) may behave like a particle in one environmental context and like a wave in another context, showing a wave-particle duality depending on the environmental context. That is vividly illustrated and proven in Richard Feynman's well-known double-slit experiment [54]. This mysterious finding has not been explained.

According to Bohm [54], this phenomenon suggests that an electron seems to have a conscious mind and act like a living organism, and seems to have consciousness interacting with the environmental background field of space. This is a transformation from a wave to a particle and vice versa like in an organism, rather than interacting parts of an inanimate machine. The electron seems to be gathering information in space about its environment and responding according to the meaning of the obtained information, showing a capacity for transformation like an organism.

Alain Aspect and his collaborators [4] (Guy Lyon Playfair, *Twin Telepathy* [56]) experimentally proved in the 1980s that the speed of transmission of mutual effect between two electron twins with the identical state generated under certain conditions and separated by twelve meters was twenty times faster than the speed of light.

In 1997, Nicolas Gisin in Geneva repeated Alain Aspect's experiment [4]. He found that communication between two particles (*e.g.*, electrons and photons that are "entangled" and have the same quantum state) ten kilometers apart appeared to be 20,000 times faster than the speed of light (Ervin Laszlo, *Science and the Akashic Field* [45]).

In 1997, Swiss researcher A. Watson successfully repeated this experiment over a distance of several miles [69].

The instantaneous influence between two electron twins violates the speed of light according to Einstein's theory of relativity.

Bohm imagines that the electron seems to be of a conscious nature with infinite speed in non-local space, exceeding the speed of light. There is no local or mechanical explanation. Einstein's relativity theory cannot explain this phenomenon, suggesting some form of non-local totality of reality, according to David Bohm (*Wholeness and Implicate Order*[10]). Nonlocality means that a particle is present not only locally but also everywhere in space at the same time.

Matter, energy, and mind are different aspects of the unknown, unbroken, flowing movement of totality; they mutually enfold and can be converted into each other. There is no separation in totality; the sense of separation is an illusion, [54].

Consciousness may be the essential nature of the universe and be a more subtle form than matter [10]. It seems to interact with subatomic particles and to be a more subtle aspect of holomovement than matter.

## Cosmic Consciousness

The deeper background beyond consciousness, matter, and energy contains hidden explicit and implicit contents of consciousness, matter, and energy. Bohm called these contents "information." Particles and antiparticles are generated as forms of real information from corresponding virtual information of the whole. Virtual information of the background of the whole is processed and transmitted to real matter, energy, and consciousness. This deeper background consciousness of Bohm seems to me to be cosmic consciousness [10].

Meditation in silence of the mind is recommended for obtaining insight into the whole, the immeasurable world. The depth of consciousness and the self are unknown [10].

## All Is in Each

The entire space of the universe is in each region of space; it is a holographic universe. A myriad of waves of matter and consciousness exist in each region of space. The above-described quantum theories of David Bohm seem to be very close to the teachings of Buddha that I remember from my childhood: *the universe is in a particle, and an eon is in a moment.*

# CHAPTER 9

# New Discoveries in Modern Science

One of the great philosophers and scientists of our modern time, Ervin Laszlo, published an outstanding book called *Science and the Akashic Field* [45]. His brilliant and comprehensive work is aimed at unifying the realms of science and consciousness in an "Integral Theory of Everything." The new discoveries in modern science described in his book are particularly interesting, fascinating, and thought-provoking for me.

In modern science, many important findings in the physical world and the realm of consciousness have been discovered and seem to be supportive of Bohm's quantum theories.

## Telepathy (Transpersonal Connection)

Guy Lyon Playfair, one of the world's leading psychic researchers, wrote a book called *Twin Telepathy* [56]. He has produced overwhelming evidence indicating a special mental connection between identical twins. The occurrence of telepathy-proneness among identical twins is between 30 and 40 percent. The success rate in telepathy seems to be dependent on the degree of the bond between sender and receiver.

Everything in the physical world appears separated in space and time; individual minds are separated and independent. In contrast, in the world of spiritual consciousness, minds of individual inner selves appear instantly and non-locally connected (Russell Targ and Jane Katra, *Miracles of Mind* [67]). The inner selves interact and exchange all information mutually. The physical self is seemingly connected with the inner self, probably through a window that performs a selective filtering or blocking function. Some people who are gifted with direct contact with or easy access to their inner selves through meditation or trance may have psychic capabilities like telepathy, clairvoyance, and precognition.

In 1988, Randolph Byrd, MD[13], wrote of the beneficial effect of intercessory prayer (praying for others) on the medical course and recovery of 393 patients with heart disease hospitalized in the coronary care unit of the University of California's San Francisco General Hospital. His data suggested that intercessory prayer had a beneficial therapeutic effect. The results of Byrd's research also seem to prove telepathic transpersonal connection between praying people and patients.

In 1999, William Harris and his collaborators [37] published the result of their research that repeated Byrd's study. A total of 990 patients with heart disease who were admitted to the coronary care unit of the Mid American Heart Institute in Kansas City, Missouri, participated in this study. Compared with the usual care group of 524 patients, the prayer group of 466 patients had significantly better hospital course scores. The results suggested that prayer was an effective adjunct to standard care. They also seem to prove telepathic transpersonal connection between praying people and patients. It seems to me that telepathic connection is carried out by the inner selves of those praying and the patients.

## Mental Connection between Man and Environment

Professional dowsers endowed with a special sensitivity are able to accurately dowse for underground water and locate veins of water, oil, gold, or other things. According to George Applegate, author of *The Complete Book of Dowsing* [2], the occurrence rate of success by the famous modern dowsers is 90 to 95 percent.

George Applegate is an engineer and considered one of the world's leading dowsers. He has been dowsing all over the world for fifty years in search of water for governments and numerous industrial companies.

Documented and proven facts about dowsing for water appear to strongly indicate a conscious connection between man and the natural environment. It also seems to me to suggest that the inner self of the dowser perceives the vibratory energy of conscious waves that originates from dowsed underground water and that comes to the subconscious mind of the dowser's the inner self like the resonance phenomenon of vibrations.

## Dream Telepathy and Precognition

Montague Ullman, Stanley Krippner, and Alan Vaughan, of the Maimonides Dream Laboratory at the Maimonides Medical Center in New York City, wrote a book called *Dream Telepathy* [68]. In it they tell that based on studies of dream telepathy (ESP) in the United States, Germany, Britain, and India, 40–60 percent of telepathic experiences were dream experiences.

In *Famous Precognitive and Problem-Solving Dreams and Others* [55], Andrew O'Loughlin wrote of numerous documented and authenticated cases, including those of Edgar Cayce's, of dreams predicting future events of death, disaster, volcano eruptions, shipwrecks, airplane crashes, crime, accidents, and so forth. He described various aspects of dreams. Precognitive dreams are mentioned in the bible (Matthew 1:18–25, 2:10–13).

The inner self in dreams enters the world of consciousness, the spiritual world that transcends space and time, and is non-local and timeless. It seems possible that the inner self can travel through the past, the present, and the future like a time machine and so can have retrocognition, simultaneous cognition, and precognition in dreams.

## General Characteristics of Dream Precognition and Telepathy

**1.** Special dreams that come true in reality are the work of the inner self while asleep.

**2.** Dream telepathy and precognition seem to be acts of the inner self in the realm of consciousness that is non-local and timeless, covering past, present, and future.

**3.** In a precognitive dream, the inner self of the dreamer seems to have telepathic communication with a spiritual entity or a radiating subtle energy wave from the environment.

**4.** In her book *The Dream Seer* [70], Cindi Welch, who was a dream investigator for two decades, wrote that time frames and dates in dreams, at least for her, had been rather unreliable.

There seem to be no cases of precognitive dreams published in books that I have read and researched that have a description of a prediction with a verbal expression or a written figure, in a dream or a trance, of an exact date when a future actual event would take place, like the thirty-first day or the thirteenth day, in the near future beyond twenty-four hours of the dream.

**5.** In a dream or a trance, the inner self of the dreamer or psychic goes out to the world of consciousness as well as the physical world, leaving

117

the physical body (known as an out-of-body experience). The inner self has all kinds of experiences, such as telepathic communication and precognition. The inner self returns to the physical body afterward and may impress the memories of experiences upon the mind of the physical self at the moment of waking.

In a similar way, in the case of a medium in a trance, the inner self of the medium goes out, and a spiritual entity comes in and controls the medium's body. There will be communication and dialogue between the spiritual entity and the sitter(s) in the audience of a session. At the end of the session, the spiritual entity goes out, and the inner self of the medium returns to the physical body. Once the inner self reenters the physical body, the physical self generally has no memory of the content of what occurred in the session.

**Near-Death Experiences (NDE)**

A friend of mine—I shall call him Jassie—was a scientist who had worked for the National Aeronautics and Space Administration in Florida. He and his wife moved to Morristown, Tennessee, after his retirement.

My wife and I were invited to dinner by the couple one evening. Jassie was brilliant and had broad scientific knowledge. He was a patriotic veteran of the U.S. Army and had fought in World War II. He was stationed in Okinawa, Japan, during the war.

That evening, Jassie told us the extraordinary story of something that he had experienced. He said he had only told his wife about it, because he thought others would say he was crazy. His story was about his near-death experience. He told us that he had not been concerned about life after death or near-death experiences before. He was not interested in paranormal phenomena.

One day, he had undergone abdominal surgery, during which he suddenly developed cardiac arrest and was clinically dead. He left his body and floated up near the ceiling of the operating room. He saw his body lying on the operating table. He could observe the medical and nursing staff working and talking around the table, and he could see anesthetic equipment and surgical instruments in the room. They were attempting resuscitation of his body. The surgeon told to his wife, "There seems to be no hope." Jassie saw and heard his wife saying, "Don't leave me alone. Please come back to life, Jassie."

Jassie saw all of this and heard all that they said while he floated above the operating table, near the ceiling. He came to after successful resuscitation procedures. He returned to his physical body.

When he recovered, he asked his wife and one nurse, who had been in the operating room at the time of his surgery, many questions about the situation in the operating room. He was astounded to find that what he saw and heard during his near-death experience was what had happened in reality. My wife and I were astonished to hear his extraordinary story of NDE, though we had already previously heard and read that kind of NDE story.

In Brad Steiger's *One with the Light* [65] and Guy Lyon Playfair's *Twin Telepathy* [56], both authors described the same extraordinary case of a near-death experience.

Both authors describe the true story of a physician. According to this anonymous physician, shortly after midnight, the doctor was stricken with acute gastroenteritis and apparently suffered a cardiac arrest and unconsciousness. He was subsequently resuscitated by another doctor. He experienced an extraordinary phenomenon during the period from the cardiac arrest to recovery. He saw two personalities, A and B, that he felt to be himself: one personality, B, linked to his body (the physical self, or ego), and the other personality, A, free from the body (the inner/super self, the true self, soul). The B personality faded and disappeared as the physical body deteriorated further. The A personality was separating from the other personality and leaving his physical body. The A personality was conscious outside the body and could observe his body lying in bed. He realized that he could also see everything in his house.

After resuscitation with a camphor injection, the A personality returned to his physical body. Once he was back, all clear vision of everything disappeared.

In the above published case of NDE, it seems most likely that what occurred was that the inner self (the A personality) left the physical body. The inner self saw the other part of the self, the physical self (the B personality); this remained attached to the body and then disintegrated as the brain and the body ceased to function; then the physical self was unconscious in the physical world. On the basis of the above true story, I infer that both the inner self and the physical self are unknowably superposed and coexist in the individual self of a man.

In near-death experiences, the inner self enters a different dimensional world of consciousness, the spiritual or psychic world that transcends time and space, being timeless and non-local. The inner self can travel instantly to anywhere it wants to go.

A near-death experience is in some ways similar to an out-of-body experience, or OBE (William Buhlman, *Adventures Beyond the Body* [14]). In both cases, the inner self temporarily leaves the physical body and later returns to the body, resuming life in the three-dimensional physical world. The difference is that in cases of NDE, the physical body temporarily stops physiological functions and is clinically dead, but in cases of OBE, the physical body continues to function and is clinically alive.

## General Characteristics of Near-Death Experiences

Many authentic cases of near-death experiences are described by the authors Brad Steiger [65], Margot Grey [34], and Sogyal Rinpoche [59]. I would like to summarize general characteristic aspects of near-death experiences after my review of some documented cases in published books.

- Near-death experiences may occur in cases of accidents, surgery, unconsciousness, coma, high fever, etc.
- Major vital organs such as heart and brain stop functioning (clinically dead) in cases of NDE.
- The inner self, the true self, leaves the physical body, floating up near the ceiling or at the corner of the room, seeing the body lying in bed or on an operating table, and in some occasions observing the physical self (the false self) attached to the body disintegrating and fading away. The inner self separates and is free from the physical body.
- The inner self enters a different dimension, a spiritual world of consciousness that transcends time and space, being timeless and non-local. The inner self can instantly travel to anywhere it desires with the power of the mind.
- The inner self can see both the spiritual and the physical world; however, the physical selves of other ordinary people cannot see the spiritual world or the inner self.
- The inner self can meet deceased relatives and friends, or spiritual entities, angels, or saints, and may have a glimpse of heaven and sometimes brilliant light (Brad Steiger, *One with the Light* [65]).
- The inner self is the true self. The physical self is the false self, impermanent and perishable; the physical self fades or regenerates, depending on functions of the body.

- The inner self feels love, happiness, peace of mind, calm, bliss, and no pain associated with the physical body.

- The inner self is made to return to the physical body when it is not the time to leave the body for good (death). This information is given to the inner self by deceased relatives, angels, or higher spiritual entities. In this situation, this process represents a case of NDE.

- If it is time to leave the body for good, then death occurs, and the inner self begins a new life after death in the spiritual world or enters the Kingdom of Heaven. If the inner self, after death, is reborn in the physical world, following a period of some length of sojourn in the spiritual world (bardo), this rebirth means reincarnation (Christopher Bache, *Life Cycles* [5]).

- The inner self may learn of the presence of the spiritual world and the Kingdom of Heaven, life after death, the imperishable soul, or the purpose of life, love, and wisdom. The lives of people who have had near-death experiences and return to their bodies are changed dramatically, and they are full of love for fellow people (Brad Steiger, *Return from Death* [34]).

- There seem to be three worlds that superpose and coexist: (1) the physical world, the lowest world; (2) the spiritual world, the inner world, the intermediate world; and (3) the celestial world, the Kingdom of Heaven, the highest world. Inhabitants of the higher worlds seem to be able to see the lower worlds, but those of the lower worlds cannot see the higher worlds, which are unknown or unknowable to them. Enlightened souls are believed to see all three worlds. God, the creator, runs the whole universe.

# PART FIVE

Coexisting Worlds of Science and Religion

# — CHAPTER 10 —

## The Physical World and the Spiritual World

A number of new discoveries have been made in modern science, in quantum physics, psychology, and parapsychology. According to the great physicist David Bohm's new quantum theories (*Wholeness and Implicate Order* [10]; Lee Nichol, *The Essential David Bohm* [55]), there is no absolute solid substance; there is no objective tangible element in the universe. There is only a process of the whole—the unknown, probably unknowable whole. There is only action of the totality, of universal, undivided, flowing movement of the whole. The process of the whole creates matter and consciousness in the reality of the universe, as described in Chapter 8.

Ervin Laszlo, a great thinker, proposed an "Integral Theory of Everything" in his book *Science and the Akashic Field* [45]. Laszlo's theory excellently describes a brilliant view toward understanding the real nature of matter and consciousness, quanta, atoms, living organisms, stars, galaxies, cosmos, and life (Chapter 9). His theory is seemingly based on the new quantum theories of David Bohm. Science has begun to acknowledge the unseen spiritual world that all saints and prophets of major world religions—Jesus, Gautama, Krishna, Confucius, and Muhammad—taught about.

The unseen realm of the spiritual world appears unknowable and unfamiliar to most ordinary people in this life on Earth. Laszlo's theory explains matter and consciousness in terms of "information," dealing with created products, forms, or processes of the whole as described by David Bohm, essentially dealing with the created but not the creator, God. The spiritual world is beyond the physical world. The two worlds appear to be of unconceivable, different dimensions or planes of energy levels, and they are superimposed and coexist. Souls are created by the creator, and at the same time, they are part of the creator.

Souls live in the spiritual world of their homeland. Souls, the inner and super selves of humans, live in the physical world, residing in physical bodies and coexisting with their physical selves.

I would like to further explore the unseen spiritual world, not on the basis of modern scientific-method-based findings, but instead on the basis of mediumship-based findings.

## Afterlife Experiments in Mediumship-Based Psychic Research

University of Arizona professor Gary Schwartz and his co-workers carried out scientific research to prove the existence of life after death with the collaboration of the five current most renowned and highly skilled psychic mediums: John Edward, Suzane Northrop, George Anderson, Anne Gehman and Laurie Campbell. He published their research data in his book *The Afterlife Experiments* [63].

Ordinary volunteer subjects were chosen as sitters in sessions of experiments and communicated, through the mediums, with their deceased relatives and friends in research laboratories with strict scientific environments and fraud-proof experimental procedures. The mediums were trustworthy, decent, and cooperative superstars.

The results they obtained were impressive. The mediums actually picked up accurate information from the spirit world using telepathy. Schwartz found that the accuracy of the five mediums ranged from 77 to 93 percent, with the total average score being 83 percent of +3 absolute accuracy [64]. According to John Edward (*Crossing Over* [28]), the 17 percent of inaccuracy was mostly due to misinterpretation of the information as symbols given by spirits; so information from the Other Side is considered accurate.

Schwartz and his co-workers published their research data in the *Journal of the Society for Psychical Research* [64], a publication devoted to the exploration of psychic phenomena.

## After-Death Communication (ADC) by John Edward, Psychic Medium

John Edward, the internationally known television medium superstar, helped thousands of his clients communicate with their deceased relatives and friends on the Other Side. He published several books, including *One Last Time* [27] and *Crossing Over* [28]. He wrote numerous unimaginable and fascinating stories related to after-death communications. According to his writings, he became fairly adept at opening and closing himself to spirit communication. He can open himself to spirit vibrations so that messages come through him more clearly. His role is to be a bridge between our physical world and the spirit world, and to deliver messages from the Other Side to the living people on this side.

I believe that John Edward's mission, as an outstanding, incredible medium on this Earth, is to prove to millions of people that our souls survive in the spiritual world after death, that love is eternal, and that our souls grow spiritually in this life and on the Other Side.

## Psychic Healing by Arigo, Brazilian Peasant

In John Fuller's book *Arigo, Surgeon of the Rusty Knife* [30], he tells a true story of an incredible Brazilian peasant, Jose Arigo (real name Jose Pedro de Freitas), who was a medium for the spirit of a deceased German doctor, Adolpho Fritz.

Thousands of patients from all over South America, North America, and Europe came to see him for treatment. He treated many known diseases, including fatal, incurable cancers of lung, liver, and ovary; leukemia; retinoblastoma; goiter; kidney disease; arthritis; backache; paraplegia; elephantiasis; allergy; hypertension; and lipoma. Diagnoses of tumors and diseases were confirmed by biopsies or the same doctors who had given up on those patients' diseases as incurable or inoperable.

Arigo was in a trance when he was treating patients. His movements were controlled by the German doctor's spirit, Dr. Fritz, who used Arigo as a vehicle and prescribed medicine and performed surgery. When Arigo woke up, he had no memory of his psychic medical and surgical healing work. He never went beyond the third grade in education, and he never studied medicine. Arigo was a faithful Catholic and a decent man.

Herculano Pires, a professor of philosophy, interviewed Arigo in a trance state. The voice of Arigo claimed that the entity who was speaking through Arigo as a channel was Dr. Fritz.

Both Brazilian and American doctors verified Arigo's healing works and took color motion pictures of his work and operations.

Arigo is comparable to Edgar Cayce, the widely known American psychic who made accurate diagnoses and gave effective prescriptions to thousands of patients from all over the world for four decades while asleep in trance. It seems to me that Cayce's incredible medical healing was done by his inner self in trance, although he did not use a knife for surgeries as Arigo did. In contrast to Cayce, Arigo was used as a medium for the spirit Dr. Fritz, who performed unbelievable medical and surgical healing for nearly two decades. Neither case of miraculous healing can be explained by modern science and medicine.

This fascinating, true story of Arigo, the Brazilian peasant and psychic healer, seems to be undeniable and valuable historical evidence of miraculous healing provided by a highly advanced spirit through a medium. It also suggests that medicine could be further developed by unceasing research with divine help.

## General Characteristics of After-Death Communication by Mediumship

- When vital functions of the brain, heart, and lungs stop, the physical self disintegrates and disappears, and the inner self, the true self (the soul), leaves the physical body and crosses over to the Other Side, the spirit world of a different plane and energy level.
- The soul, the inner self, continues to live after death as a spirit, with all past memories of its experiences in its life on Earth.
- The medium is gifted with the ability to telepathically communicate with dead personalities and receive and interpret information from the Other Side.
- The spiritual world on the Other Side is a place of peace and beauty (John Edward, *One Last Time* [27]).
- Spirits continue to strive, grow, and unfold after death (John Edward [27]).
- Mediums communicate with the Other Side in an altered state of consciousness: in a state of meditation or a trancelike state.
- Each person has a spirit guide or guides during a life on Earth (John Edward [27]). The guide is an advanced, higher spirit.

- Dreams are a primary venue for spirit communication, a spirit's way of visiting this world and directly communicating with people (John Edward [27])

- We are not punished on the Other Side, but instead by ourselves (John Edward [27]). The inner self (spirit) seeks to improve and evolve.

- Free will is respected and not infringed. Spirits have their own will but do not try to force sitters or mediums. They try to make people understand and voluntarily agree with their opinions by means of transmitting necessary information to sitters and mediums (John Edward [27]).

- The life of a soul and love are eternal. The purpose of after-death communication is to prove this fact (John Edward [27]).

- Time and space have no meaning in the spiritual world. The inner self has a non-local mind that transcends space and time.

- Brain first or consciousness first? Here are my thoughts:
  - The brain is first, and consciousness of the physical self is second. The brain generates the consciousness of the physical self. When the brain is anesthetized, in a coma, or dead, the consciousness of the physical self disintegrates and disappears.
  - The consciousness of the inner self, the true self, and the creator is first, and the brain, the non-self, is second, because the brain is created by the creator, the totality of inner selves that are part of the creator (Chapters 5, 7).

- On the basis of the true story of Arigo's miraculous psychic medical and surgical healing capabilities, a highly advanced medical spirit or saint can help a medium in a trance perform inexplicable, miraculous medical and surgical procedures on patients, by using the medium as a vehicle and commanding his body. This story is incomprehensible but undeniable evidence of the physical world and the spiritual world coexisting!

## Religions

1. All religions are essentially saying the same teachings. All different religions lead to one point: All souls are connected and one with our creator god. As Jesus said, "Holy Father, protect them by the power of your name—the name you gave me—so that they may be one, as we are one" (John 17:11).

2. Religions are based on the teaching that we are constantly striving to reach higher levels of spirituality (John Edward [27]). All is interconnected in the universe. Divine love is the great power that moves everything in the universe. Our souls come to this Earth to learn love and compassion.

3. Findings in modern science and all religions lead us to conclude that the physical world and the spiritual world are superimposed and coexist. They are of different energy levels and dimensions. The physical world has time and space. The spiritual world is timeless and non-local.

4. In the physical world, if the cause is known, the effect may be predictable on the basis of the law of cause and effect. In the spiritual world, if the effect (the idea) is known, the cause (the "information") may be recognizable or creatable on the basis of the law (anti-law) of effect and cause.

# — Chapter 11 —

## My Personal Psychic Experiences and Contemplation

I believe in teachings of Eastern and Western saints, Gautama Buddha, Jesus Christ, Krishna, Confucius, Kim Il Bu, and other saints. I would believe data on results of fraud-proof, trustworthy scientific research experiments (Gary E. Schwartz, *The Afterlife Experiments* [64]). I surely believe in my own direct experiences in my life.

I would like to describe my own actual psychic experiences and my relevant contemplation and personal interpretation on the basis of my present beliefs and knowledge.

### Pleurisy Treated by My Father in My Childhood

I left my parents and my hometown, Pohang, for the first time in order to attend Kyungbuk Middle School at Taegu City, about fifty miles away. One spring day when I was in seventh grade, I suddenly developed high fever, headache, shortness of breath, and malaise. I was lying in a boarding house room away from school. My consciousness got vague and confused. My cousin happened to visit and found me very sick with high fever. He called a doctor for a patient home visit. The doctor made a diagnosis of acute pleurisy with fluid in the chest.

He aspirated a few cubic centimeters of pleural fluid with a syringe (see Chapter 1).

My cousin told the doctor that my father, Hwa Kee Chung, was a doctor practicing in my home town, Pohang. He placed a long-distance call to my father, informing him of my severe illness of acute pleurisy with fluid in the chest. My father told him, "I already knew that Sung Jang is suffering pleurisy with fluid in the chest. Bring him immediately to Pohang by taxi."

I returned home to Pohang after about two hours in a taxi. I recall that an old lady who was a close friend of my mother often visited our home in my middle-school and high-school days. She was a medium who could communicate with a spirit known to her. The medium had visited my parents that day, before my father got a long-distance call from my cousin. She told my parents, "Sung Jang in Taegu is suffering an illness, with fluid in the chest." My parents were shocked to hear the message from the spirit through the medium. They became worried and anxious. The medium left our home after giving her message. Soon after she left, the long-distance call reached my parents.

My father confirmed the diagnosis of acute exudative pleurisy by physical examination. He decided to have me withdraw from school temporarily and to treat me himself at home.

The next day, my father examined me and aspirated about one liter of straw-colored pleural fluid with a special large syringe. I took daily medical treatments with oral drugs, intravenous medication, and absolute bed rest.

A few days passed, and by physical examination, my father found that chest fluid had accumulated again. He told us his findings. Our family discussed it and wished that it would be better to treat my pleurisy with medication, without repeat aspiration of chest fluid by using a large, thick needle. My parent felt that a repeat aspiration would be a painful procedure for me.

My mother asked the spirit a question in a session when the lady medium visited that day. She said, "Sung Jang has a large amount of accumulated fluid in his chest again. What can we do? We wish to continue the current treatment without any more aspiration, if possible."

Immediately, the spirit spoke using the medium's voice and answered, "If you feel it is pitiful to do a repeat aspiration of the chest fluid, leave him without it, and wait. Do not worry."

My father listened to the spirit's message and told us that he has made up his mind not to perform a repeat aspiration of the chest fluid, but instead to wait and observe me.

The following day my father re-examined me by auscultation and percussion. He was really astounded to find that the large amount of accumulated chest fluid was completely gone! There was no need of a repeat aspiration. Furthermore, I did not need to undergo another thoracentesis until my complete recovery from pleurisy.

I would like to propose the following things:

- An advanced spirit can make a diagnosis in the physical body of a human being.
- A spirit entity can transmit findings or information through a medium's voice to us living in the physical world.
- An advanced spirit can perform medical treatments on patients, like the deceased German doctor's spirit, Dr. Fritz, cured thousands of patients' illness using the medium Arigo, a Brazilian peasant, as a vehicle (John G. Fuller, *Arigo: Surgeon of the Rusty Knife* [31]) (see Chapter 10).

## Story of Carp

There is an unusual, interesting story related to carp from when I was sick with pleurisy in my childhood, as described in Chapter 1. The spring of the seventh grade, when my father's treatment had begun, was gone, and the hot summer came. My father's sister's husband went fishing in nearby Hyungsan River when he had free time. If he could catch even a few carp, he would walk to our house with them. He gave the carp to us in order to help my nutritional diet therapy. Carp soup in summer was a valuable nutritional diet for patients.

We had a severe drought that summer. One early morning the lady medium visited our home and said, "I have come here early this morning because the spirit asked me to come to Sung Jang's home and give you some information." She continued, speaking for the spirit, "The water gate of the lake behind the mountains west of the City of Pohang was opened this morning to drain the lake water in order to supply water to dry rice fields and farmland in drought. Crowds of people have gathered there. There are lots of carp in the water flowing out. Go quickly, and catch them for a nutritional supplement for Sung Jang."

My parent sent our two employees to the lake. They encountered the exact same scene that the spirit had described. About two hours later, they came home with buckets full of many carp that they had caught at the lake.

My whole family was greatly astonished to see them in reality. Scores of carp were placed in the small pond in our courtyard.

They planned to keep the carp alive in the pond, to be used for the purpose of my nutritional diet therapy. The scores of carp were vigorously swimming and moving around in the pond.

The next morning, my family went to see how the carp were doing in the pond. Unexpectedly, almost all of the carp were upside down, showing their bellies, and motionless. Such changes in their posture and behavior might indicate that the carp suffered severe stress from being caught by human hands, transportation from the lake to our home in a bucket, and the new environment of our pond. The carp might have carried disease from the lake and developed the above-described abnormal signs on that day for the first time.

My whole family was concerned and worried about the possible death of all the carp. The lady medium visited our home that day. My mother told this fact to the spirit in our session. The spirit replied, through the medium, "Do not worry about the carp. Just keep them in the pond and use them for a nutritional diet food."

My family listened to the spirit's answer and decided to continue keeping the carp in the pond.

The next morning, my worried family went to the pond in order to see how the carp were doing. A wonderful phenomenon had occurred. None of the carp were found dead! The scores of carp were lively, moving around in the pond.

- It seems to me most likely that the spirit actually helped the carp adapt to the new environment and recover from their ill condition. This seems to me to be possible if I take into consideration that the deceased German doctor's spirit, Dr. Fritz, cured many patients. This might be also comparable to Dr. William Braud's findings (Russell Targ and Jane Katra, *Miracles of Mind* [68]) that a person directly influenced the behavior of remote living systems, using mental means alone; the experiment revealed mental influence on the spontaneous swimming behavior of small knife fish (a kind of carp). (See Chapter 9.) In this case, the difference is a human mind's influence and a spirit's power.

- A spirit entity can give information on the physical world to sitters through a medium in a session.

- The spirit once said in a session, "Spirits can instantaneously go anywhere, regardless of the distance, if they want to." This statement means that the spiritual world on the Other Side is non-local and timeless.

- The physical world and the spiritual world are superimposed and coexist in reality.

## A Precognitive Dream in Prison

In 1944, Korea was under the suppressive colonial Japanese government. I was a medical student at Keijo Imperial University College of Medicine (now the Seoul National University College of Medicine). I joined a student underground organization for Korea's independence movement. The movement was detected by the Japanese police. I was arrested by the police in December 1944. I was imprisoned after interrogation and inhumane torture in Seodaemun Prison in Seoul in January 1945 (see Chapter 2).

Harshly cold wind blew directly into the prison cell with high, broken windows. The room temperature was probably -10° C (14° F). It was freezing cold. Epidemic typhus fever prevailed in Seodaemun Prison that winter of 1944–5, infecting many prisoners. I heard that quite a number of patients died of typhus. I was one of the patients, and I was placed in an isolation room without any medical treatment for months. I suffered high fever, headache, complete loss of appetite, loss of hearing, malaise, vague consciousness, and a seemingly comatose state. I cannot recall how many months I spent in the isolation ward. But my fever eventually came down, and my consciousness came back, as well as my hearing. I was moved out of the isolation ward to a cell where five or six accused detainees were accommodated; it was probably

May 1945. I was glad to join relatively healthy-looking people in the cell. I began to feel gradual recovery of my stamina from the weakened physical condition I had suffered due to severe typhus fever.

One night in June 1945, I had an unusual dream. An old man in a gray Korean coat *(durumagi)* suddenly appeared in front of me in my dream. I fell to the ground face down and asked him, "When shall I be released from prison?"

He answered instantly, "**The day is the thirty-first.**" Then the old man disappeared, and at the same time, I woke up from the extraordinary dream. I believed that I had experienced a precognitive dream, and I began to wait for the thirty-first day of July. About one month later, I was unexpectedly released from prison on the exactly predicted day, July 31, 1945. Fifteen days later, my motherland, Korea, was liberated from the thirty-five-year Japanese colonial occupation by the Allied forces in World War II and regained independence on August 15, 1945.

I have believed throughout my life that the special dream in the prison in June 1945 was a revelation from heaven. After having studied religions and science regarding life and nature, and having gone through many ups and downs in my life, I have come to believe that an advanced spirit—probably a spirit guide, a saint, or my ancestor—appeared in my dream in prison and predicted the coming date of my release. The spirit really visited me in my dream and had telepathic communication with my inner self. Whenever I think of the unusual dream, inexpressible joy, wonder, faith, and gratitude for God's grace fill my heart.

## A Precognitive Dream in North Korea during the Korean War

In 1950, when North Korea invaded South Korea, I was one of hundreds of South Korean physicians who were forcefully transported from Seoul to North Korea by North Korean communist agents (see Chapter 3). My group of six South Korean physicians was sent to Hamhung, North Korea and ordered to treat patients at the Hamhung Provincial Hospital. I was assigned to the Department of Medicine to treat general civilian outpatients. Inpatients were treated by other physicians. These inpatients included North Korean civilian and military patients.

Air raids involving machine-gun strafing by U.S. fighter planes and bombing by scores of U.S. B-29 bombers in formation were daily getting more severe. During the daytime, whenever siren signals of air raid were heard, we had to stop medical service work and immediately seek refuge in an air-raid shelter. In those days, the circumstances during daylight hours did not allow medical staff to practice medical service activities because U.S. air raids were so frequent.

One night in September 1950, I had an unusual dream. I saw a wall calendar with a black printed number of the date in the middle of the rectangular, white paper. The number was a crystal-clear **13**. That seemed to indicate that the date of the coming thirteenth day— of October—would be an especially important and critical day. The calendar then disappeared, and I saw a night scene. In the darkness of night, I was walking toward one direction with other people in a line.

I looked around both sides of the road. There was a flowing river on the left side, and a mountain on the right side. I said to a nearby nurse, "If we pass the thirteenth day tonight, we will survive and have good days ahead. Let's be patient. We have hope."

The nurse appeared glad to hear me say it. After talking to the nurse, I woke up. I felt that the thirteenth day would be the coming October 13. I began to wait for that day. I believed that if I passed October 13 without any difficult events, I would have good days thereafter. I had a good reason to believe and wait for the thirteenth day of October, on the basis of my previous experience of an unusual precognitive dream

I'd had in prison in June 1945, when Korea was under Japanese colonial occupation. I had dreamed the date of my release from prison, and it had come true. Therefore, I believed that the dream in North Korea was a second revelation from heaven in my life.

The great historical battle at Inchon Harbor involving the landing by UN and ROK forces on September 15, 1950; recapture of the capital, Seoul, on September 27–8; crossing the 38$^{th}$ parallel on October 9; and the northward advance of UN and ROK forces, totally changed the situation of the war in the Korean peninsula (Leif A. Gruenberg, *Defining Moments: The Korean War* [36]).

The long-awaited day of October 13 came. An unexpected event took place. The Communist agent responsible for the hospital ordered the entire staff of Hamhung Provincial Hospital to gather at the hospital campus that evening to prepare to retreat north. Scores of North and South Korean doctors, nurses, and non-medical staff members started to retreat north on foot in a formation of lines and groups, leaving the hospital and Hamhung City behind in the darkness of night.

I got out of Hamhung City for the first time. All of the hospital personnel were walking in line on a dark road leading north. I looked around at the surrounding natural scene while I walked. The Chungjin River was on my left side. and mountains were on my right. It was an amazing event. The night scene and the date exactly matched the landscape and the number thirteen on the wall calendar in my dream a few weeks earlier. The coincidence of the dream and the reality was unbelievable beyond expression and convinced me to believe that the special dream was a precognitive dream and a revelation from heaven.

I spoke to a nurse who was walking beside me, as I had in my dream. I said, "Hello. If we pass the thirteenth day tonight, we will be free. Let's be patient tonight. We will have good days starting from tomorrow." The nurse was glad to hear me say it. I did not tell her about my dream. I just talked similarly to how I had done in my dream. I felt inexpressible joy and hope while I was walking. My heart was pounding with gratitude, wonder, and courage.

The scene and experience in reality on the night of October 13, 1950, together with the extraordinary dream of revelation, have been living in my mind as invaluable memories for more than fifty years.

I now feel that my inner self most likely foresaw telepathically, in my dream state, the near-future scene of special events in the spiritual world that is non-local and timeless, perceiving subtle energy "information" waves in nature just as dowsers feel the presence of underground water, oil, or gold.

## The Meeting of My Mother and My Future Wife at Pusan, Korea

During the Korean War, in October 1950, I returned to South Korea from North Korea, where I had been forcibly transported by invading North Korean communist agents. Escape from North Korea by crossing the fierce battle line was impossible and unimaginable, but I had a narrow escape from death with God's grace and help. In North Korea, I was alone, separated from my family as well as my love, Miss Kwang Jun Lee, who would be my fiancée and wife. I came back and met my parents at Pohang, Kyungbuk. I did not know whereabouts of Miss Lee. She was a medical student at the Soodo Women's Medical School (now the Korea University College of Medicine). She lived with her parents in Seoul when the Korean War broke out in June 1950. My parents had heard from me about Miss Lee but had not yet met her. They knew that I loved her very much. We did not hear any news of her until several months after my return from North Korea in October 1950.

One day, a nurse from Pohang visited our home on her vacation. She told us that Miss Lee was working at the Republic of Korea Third

Army Hospital in Pusan, where she worked. My parents and I were so glad to hear of Miss Lee, and we wanted to see her as soon as we could. My parents were quite curious and anxious to get to know their potential future daughter-in-law.

At that time I worked as a civilian employee for the U.S. Army Supply Depot at Taegu City. One day while I was at work, I suddenly wanted to see Miss Lee. I could get a permission for two days' leave, and I took a bus headed for Pusan. I got to Pusan after about two hours of riding in the bus. I made my way to the Third Army Hospital.

I was surprised to find my mother and aunt sitting in front of the gate of the army hospital, and I greeted them with joy and surprise. They said that they had just arrived at the hospital a few minutes before I got there and that they had asked the gate guard to arrange a meeting with Miss Kwang Jun Lee and been waiting for her.

My mother and aunt had come from Pohang, hundreds of miles away from Pusan, without informing me of their trip to see Miss Lee. None of us had anticipated seeing each other at the army hospital at that moment!

Miss Lee showed up after a while and met us with joy. She met my mother and aunt for the first time in her life. My joy was certainly beyond expression.

I have been thinking since that this unusual, unexpected encounter of three parties coming from distant cities could hardly be explained. But I would like to explain it as telepathic communication among our inner selves. This seems to be proof of a non-local, mind-to-mind connection among people with a strong bond.

Miss Lee and I got married on July 4, 1953. We celebrated our fifty-fourth wedding anniversary on Independence Day this year (2007). My son's family took us to Hawaii to celebrate our anniversary this summer. I thank God.

## An Experience on Mount Kyeryong (鷄龍山) in Korea

There is a sacred mountain named Mount Kyeryong in Choongnam-Do Province, where a Korean scholar, Kim Hang (金恒, 1826–98) was born and grew up. He studied all of the Confucian scriptures and ancient Chinese classic books. He achieved enlightenment after eighteen years' effort at the age of fifty-four years in 1879. Confucius appeared in his dream and congratulated him upon the completion of the work that Confucius had intended to finish, and he called Kim Hang "Il Bu" (一夫). Confucius admired Kim Hang for his accomplishments. Kim Hang became an avatar, an enlightened saint, and published his book *Jeong Yeok* (正易, *Right Changes*). "Il Bu" was a master of Confucianism, Buddhism, and Taoism.

His disciples continued to follow his teachings after his death in 1898. One day when I was a young man, I was advised by one of my close friends, Dr. Chong Chul Yook (陸鐘澈; Hwa Gong, 和公), to go to Mount Kyeryong and study the *Jeong Yeok.* Dr. Yook was a brilliant scientist and later studied at Argonne National Laboratory in Argonne, Illinois. After returning to Korea, he became a professor of atomic engineering at a university in Seoul. We went there and joined other disciples for one week, staying at a house owned by Cheol Hwa Song (Jeong Kwan, 貞觀). The house was located beside two large rocks, one shaped like a dragon and the other like a turtle, called the Dragon Rock and the Turtle Rock, at Kooksa Peak on Mount Kyeryong. The residence was used for disciples to study the *Jeong Yeok* and the *I Ching* of Chinese philosophy. Kim Hang spent his later life at this place (Jeong Ho Yi [72]).

Dr. Jeong Ho Yi (李正浩; Hak San, 鶴山), who was a professor of philosophy at a university and later became president of Choongnam National University and president of the Jeong Yeok Society in Korea, was among the disciples and a leading *Jeong Yeok* and *I Ching* scholar.

143

He published many outstanding books (written in Korean) related to the *Jeong Yeok* and the *I Ching*. We spent most of the time doing meditation, prayer, mantras, and *yeongga-moodo* (詠 歌 舞 蹈) day and night, except for five hours' sleep, mealtimes, and short periods of rest.

The landlord, Cheol Hwa Song, was a middle-aged, decent, and extraordinary teacher and also an amazing spirit medium. When he entered his trance state and began to speak, we disciples silently listened to his fluent, eloquent, fascinating, and sometimes poetic and beautiful speech. We were astounded and overwhelmed with wonder, joy, and faith.

We realized who was speaking from the Other Side because they identified themselves by their names: Chyeonjo-Sang Jye (天 祖 上 帝), the creator god; Soochyeon Sang Jye (樹 天 上 帝), Jesus Christ; Confucius; Kim Il Bu (金 一 夫); and Chung Po'eun (鄭 圃 隱) separately appeared and delivered lectures, giving wonderful teachings in ethics, morality, religion, and philosophy, most emphatically in love and compassion.

Tears were flowing down my cheeks, and my heart was pounding with respect, awe, gratitude, joy, and faith.

God said, "A miserable-looking, hungry beggar clothed in rags is standing at the gate in a rainy day. I am within him. I cry for him" [75]. God taught us to respect and love our neighbors as Our Father in heaven loves us. The following teachings were also given by other saints:

"Before those who govern the people perform a religious service, look around the country to see if anyone starves. Make sure that no one is starving."

"If people starve for one day, bloody tears flow for three days."

"Those who govern the people let people live in lofty buildings and large houses."

"Keep your mind as broad as the universe."

I believe that Christianity and Confucianism, as well as other major religions of the world, teach the same thing, love, and that they are multiple paths that lead us up to the mountaintop of our Father, the creator, God.

# PART SIX

## A New Philosophy of Confucius and Kim Hang

## — CHAPTER 12 —

# The Coming of a New World of Kim Hang

A scholar, Kim Hang (金恒), who was a Korean philosopher and a saint (1826–98), published his book *Jeong Yeok* (正易, *Right Changes*) in 1885 (Jeong Ho Yi, 정 역, *Jeong Yeok* [43] ; *The Third Yeok Hak* [76]). He saw the truth of the universe at the age of fifty-four after his utmost effort of study and meditation for eighteen years. He foresaw the coming new age and the new world. He wrote what he saw. In his book, Kim Hang, called "Il Bu" (一夫, "One Man"), completed the work that Confucius, a Chinese philosopher and saint (551–479 BC), started but did not finish. Kim Hang said that he wrote what heaven dictated.

I carried with me a copy of the *Jeong Yeok* during the two-month period of my stay in North Korea, where I had been forcefully transported at an early stage of the Korean War in 1950. My belief and faith in the *Jeong Yeok* gave me strength, courage, and guidance. I would like to describe humbly what I have learned and understand myself from my study of the *Jeong Yeok*, carefully avoiding any misunderstanding, prejudice, or dogmatism.

## The New Age and the New World

It is not told in his book when and how the new age and the new world will come. However, Kim Hang described the new world, the new heaven and earth, and the new human society that would come, following the universal laws. He explained the universal laws in the ancient Oriental terms of the ten *kan* (干, heavenly stems), the twelve *chi* (支, earthly branches), the sixty *kap ja* (甲 子, sixty combinations of *kan* and *chi*), the sixty-four hexagrams (卦), yin and yang, the five elements (行), the eight trigrams, the Ha Do (Ho T'u, 河 圖) Map, and the Lak Seo (Lo Shu, 洛 書) Writing (James Legge, *The I Ching* [49]; Richard Willhelm, *The I Ching or Book of Changes* [72]). The universal laws seem to be fundamentally mathematical and truly beyond my comprehension. It seems to me that avatars, enlightened sages, understand the real meaning of the universal laws. I feel that the universal laws might correspond to the unknown (probably unknowable) laws of the whole, as the great physicist David Bohm said in his book *Wholeness and the Implicate Order* [10] (Lee Nichols, *The Essential David Bohm* [54]).

The ten *kan*, the twelve *chi,* and the sixty *kap ja* are used in lunar calendars to name the year, month, day, and hour of day. The use of these terms is quite convenient in handling and expressing these items, although there would be are variations in their names.

It is said in the bible, "In the beginning was the Word, and the Word was with God, and the Word was God. All things were made by him; and without him was not anything made that has been made" (John 1:1, 3).

In mathematics, the letters $e$ and $\pi$ are used as symbols to represent certain numbers that have special meaning. These Chinese characters or words seemingly represent information, facts, and truth. It seems to me that the *kan* and *chi* likewise are used to represent information, facts, and truth in lunar calendars in the Orient.

If all things predicted in the *Jeong Yeok* happened in the coming age of the later heaven, a month would be exactly thirty days and one year 360 days, expressed with integers without fractions. Integers can be seen in nature, such as the number of petals of beautiful flowers. It seems to me that the Earth, moon, and sun would mature, and then their movements would be expressed in integers too. The thirty days of the month and 360 days of the year are exactly multiples of ten, twelve, and sixty. Consequently, the names of the months and days of a year would be fixed if expressed in terms of *kan* and *chi*. For example, the first month of any year would be named *myo* (卯); New Year's Day, January 1, would be always named *kye mi* (癸未).

The first day of any month would be *kye mi* (癸未) or *kye chook* (癸丑); the sixteenth day of any month would be *moo jeen* (戊辰) or *moo sool* (戊 戌). The time of midnight of any day would be named *hae* (亥).

In the later heaven, the ten *kan* (干): *kap* (甲), *eul* (乙), *byung* (丙), *jeong* (丁), *moo* (戊), *ki* (己), *kyung* (庚), *sin* (辛), *yim* (壬), and *kye* (癸); the twelve *chi* (支): *ja* (子), *chook* (丑), *yin* (寅), *myo* (卯), *jeen* (辰), *sa* (巳), *oh* (午), *mi* (未), *shin* (申), *yoo* (酉), *sool* (戌), and *hae* (亥); and the sixty *kap ja* (甲 子, combinations of *kan* and *chi)*, seem to be the best and the most appropriate terms or *a priori* words through the gate of which movements of the sun, Earth, and moon may be studied in the future calendar or astronomy of the solar system.

For example, the *ki* (己) position stands for the *Moogeuk* (无 極, Wu Chi), the Non-Ultimate, the Creator God; the *moo* (戊) position stands for the *Hwanggeuk* (皇 極, Huang Chi), the Ultimate Emperor, a sage. It seems to me that the positions *ki* and *moo* are non-local. The term "Original Heavenly Fire" (原 天 火) represents the creative power of the *Moogeuk*, the Creator God, and seems to express the infinite virtual energy of wholeness from the point of view of David Bohm's new quantum theories. The Original Heavenly Fire generates earth-soil (土) that seems to correspond to basic elements of matter. Yin and yang represent fundamental negative and positive forces such as the electromagnetic force, male and female, day and night, etc. The five *heng* (行)—earth-soil (土), metal (金), water (水), wood (木), and fire (火)—represent cosmic elementary, electromagnetic-like forces that seem to be "information," being creative, persistent, and changing. All things are created with the *Taegeuk* (太 極, T'ai Chi), the Great Ultimate, yin-yang; and the five *heng* (行), primordially by the *Moogeuk* (无 極), the Creator God.

The Original Heavenly Fire generates earth-soil (土); earth-soil generates metal (金); metal generates water (水); water generates wood (木); wood generates fire (火); and fire generates earth-soil (土). It seems to me macroscopically and cosmologically imaginable and comparable to the above-described processes that a Big Bang (Stephen Hawking [41]), the Original Heavenly Fire (原天火) of an unknown form of energy would have generated a myriad of elemental particles composed of energy (earth-soil, 土)—subatomic elements, quarks, antiquarks, photons, electrons, positrons, protons, neutrons, mesons, atoms, hydrogen, helium, etc.—that would have contracted and eventually produced stars (the burning of helium producing carbon, nitrogen, and oxygen in the centers of stars), the sun, the Earth, and the moon. The earth-soil (土) would have generated metal (金)—metallic atoms, iron, copper, silver, gold, etc. Metal (金) then would have generated oceans and rainwater (水); water would have generated living organisms (木) that evolved into plants, animals, and finally man; and living organisms (木) would generate earth-soil (土) through decay or incineration with heat and fire (火).

The metal-to-fire change mentioned in the *Jeong Yeok* means extraordinary, unique, transitional changes from the earlier heaven to the later heaven that is predicted by transition from the *Lak Seo* (洛 書,

the Writing from the River Lo, the *River Writing*) to the *Ha Do* (河 圖, the Yellow River Map, the *River Map*).

The *Moogeuk* (无 極, Wu Chi), expressed by the number ten, and the *Taegeuk* (太 極, T'ai Chi), expressed by the number one, are oneness. All things are made by the *Moogeuk* and the *Taegeuk*. It seems to me that this relationship might be symbolically and mathematically imaginable as follows. A logarithm with a base of 1 is used:

$$\text{Log } 1^0 = 0$$
$$\text{Log } 1^1 = 1$$
$$\text{Log } 1^2 = 2$$
$$\text{Log } 1^3 = 3$$
$$\text{Log } 1^n = n$$
$$\text{Log } 1^\infty = \infty$$
$$\text{Log } 1^\infty = \log 1 = 1$$
$$\therefore \infty = 1$$

Therefore, $0 = 1 = \infty$. As David Bohm said, "All is in one; one is in all." God is immanent and transcendent. There is no separation. Separation is illusion.

The old preceding age and world ("the earlier heaven") are symbolically represented by the *Bok Hui* (伏 羲) Eight Trigrams (the Fu Hsi Pa Kua, Figure 3) and the *Mun Wang* (文 王) Eight Trigrams (the King Wen Pa Kua, Figure 4) and the *Lak Seo* (洛書) Writing (Figure 2) as well as the *Chou Yeok* (周 易, *I Ching*). The coming new age and the new world ("the later heaven") are expressed by the symbol of the *Jeong Yeok* (正 易) Eight Trigrams (Figure 5) and the *Ha Do* (河圖) Map (Figure 2) as well as the *Jeong Yeok* (the Third Yeok called by Jeong Ho Yi ). The sets of eight trigrams are designated by different octagonal arrangements of eight trigrams.

The different diagrams of eight trigrams appear to symbolically imply historically active nations of the east, west, north, and south of the world in different ages. The old preceding age is characterized by being mutually destructive and the new age by being mutually supportive to life in humanity, as expressed by the *Mun Wang* (文王) and the *Jeong Yeok* (正易) Eight Trigrams, respectively.

If we carefully observe the *Mun Wang* (文王) Eight Trigrams (Figure 4), each trigram faces a trigram on the opposite side that is of the same gender, yin or yang in terms of number, with a feature of centrifugal expansion and growth, suggesting repulsion, as between two identical electromagnetic poles, further suggesting separation, disharmony, disorder, and mutual destruction in the earlier heaven. On the contrary, in the *Jeong Yeok* (正易) Eight Trigrams (Figure 5), each trigram faces a trigram of the other gender, yin or yang in terms of number, with a feature of centripetal attraction, suggesting mutual attraction like electromagnetic attractive forces between two different poles, and further suggesting harmony, order, equality, cooperation, and mutual support in the coming later heaven.

These phenomena are also observable in the *Ha Do* (河圖) and the *Lak Seo* (洛書) (Figure 2). In the *Lak Seo*, 4-9 metal is in the south; 2-7 fire in the west; 1-6 in the north; and 3-8 wood in the east, indicating displacement of 4-9 and 2-7 from west and south, their original, correct positions, respectively, suggesting disorder. Further, each of their numbers faces same gender number: 1-9, 2-8, 3-7, and 4-6, suggesting repulsion in the earlier heaven. In addition, the four odd heaven numbers 1, 3, 7, and 9 are at the middle positions of north, east, west, and south; the four even earth numbers 2, 4, 6, and 8 are at the corner positions of southwest, southeast, northwest, and northeast. These arrangements are suggestive of the suppression of yin and respect of yang in the earlier heaven. In the *Ha Do*, 4-9 metal and 2-7 fire return to west and south, their original, correct positions, respectively, indicating changes in their metal and fire positions; 1-6 water is in the north and 3-8 wood in the east, further showing perfect combinations of odd heaven numbers and even earth numbers in pairs in their arrangements of positions, suggesting attraction, maturation, completion, cooperation, peace, and mutual support in the coming later heaven.

*Chou Yeok* (周易, *I Ching*) is composed of the Text of the Sixty-Four Hexagrams and the Ten Wings (翼). The *I Ching* (James Legge, *The I Ching* [48]) existed in the time of Confucius. It is said that the *I Ching* was originated by the Emperor Fu Hsi (伏羲), who lived about five thousand years ago, and that it was expanded with descriptions by King Wen (文王) and his son, the Duke of Chou (周). Confucius studied the *I Ching* in the late years of his life and added the Ten Wings (翼) of his commentaries to the existing *I Ching*.

Kim Hang was the first man in history who discovered that Confucius had foreseen the coming new *Jeong Yeok* (正 易) Eight Trigrams and clearly described the specific octagonal arrangement of the eight trigrams, as illustrated in Figure 5. Kim Hang actually saw the completely new *Jeong Yeok* Eight Trigrams in a vision; it was yet unknown to scholars and not described in any book. Then he made efforts to search and find it in books, particularly in the *I Ching*. To his surprise, he found Confucius's description in the Discussion of the Trigrams (設 卦傳), Chapter II (Jeong Ho Yi [76]; James Legge [49]; Richard Willhelm [72]). The words and sentences of Confucius's description of a new arrangement of eight trigrams were found to be understandable and explicated in view of the *Jeong Yeok* Eight Trigrams.

Confucius did not publicly mention the coming new world, but he foretold it in his writing in the *I Ching* as above described and believed it himself, as Kim Hang wrote in the *Jeong Yeok*.

The *I Ching* begins with the hexagram *keon* (乾) and ends with the hexagram *mi jae* (未 濟), for a total of sixty-four hexagrams. There are no descriptions of the *Moogeuk* (无 極) or *Hwanggeuk* (皇 極) or the numbers ten and five in the *I Ching*. Ten is missing in the *Lak Seo* (洛 書). Numbers one to ten are all present in the *Jeong Yeok*.

In the *Jeong Yeok* it says that there are eight hexagrams: *bi* (否), standstill; *tae* (泰), peace; *sohn* (損), decrease; *ik* (益), increase; *ham* (咸), influence; *hang* (恒), duration; *ki jae* (既 濟), after completion; and *mi jae* (未 濟), before completion, in description of the earlier and later heavens. In four hexagrams: heaven/earth *bi* (否), standstill; mountain/lake *sohn* (損), decrease; thunder/wind *hang* (恒), duration; and fire/water *mi jae* (未 濟), before completion, trigrams that are supposed to be at the upper position exist above trigrams that are supposed to be at the lower positions, suggesting separation, repulsion, exclusion, and mutual destruction in the earlier heaven without harmony or peaceful exchange. In the other four hexagrams, earth/heaven *tae* (泰), peace; lake/mountain *ham* (咸), influence; wind/thunder *ik* (益), increase; and water/fire *ki jae* (既 濟), after completion, trigrams that are supposed to be at the upper positions move down and stay below those trigrams that are supposed to be at the lower positions and that move up above the other paired trigrams, suggesting attraction, exchange, cooperation, union, and mutual support in the later heaven.

The *yeok* (易) seems to be both metaphysical and physical science, especially astronomy, which describes and handles movements of the Earth, moon, sun, stars, and constellations.

Many stars and constellations were discovered by ancient Chinese scholars. Some major, important stars and constellations are represented and expressed by the ancient Chinese Twenty-Eight Lodges (宿), which is the oldest chart enduring up to this day, according to Frank Ross, Jr.

(*Oracles, Bones, Stones and Wheelbarrows: Ancient Chinese Science and Technology* [60]).

A list of correlations between the names of the Twenty-Eight Lodges and the names of Western reference stars is available (Christopher Cull, *Astronomy and Mathematics in Ancient China: Zhou bi suan jing*; [24]; Frank Ross [60]). The celestial sphere of 360° is divided into twenty-eight divisions along the meridian in the Twenty-Eight Lodges (宿). For example, the star *Chin* (軫, "Axletree") corresponds to γ Corvi; *Jang* (張, "Spread") to μ Hydrae; *Sam* (參, "Triaster") to α Orionis; *Myo* (昴, "Mane") to 17 Tauri; *Shil* (室, "House") to η Pegasi; *Doo* (斗, "Dipper") to φ Sagittarii; *Sim* (心, "Heart") to α Scorpii; *Hang* (亢, "Gullet") to κ Virginis; and *Kak* (角, "Horn") to α Virginis.

The Twenty-Eight Lodges (宿, *Soo*) are included in the *Jeong Yeok* (正易). As Frank Ross wrote in his book *The Stars,* when American astronauts voyaged to the moon, the ancient Chinese equatorial-coordinate method was a key element in their system of navigation for the positioning of stars [60].

Figure 1 illustrates a star chart of the Twenty-Eight Lodges and corresponding Western reference stars. The second inner and the outermost circles show stars of the Twenty-Eight Lodges and corresponding Western reference stars, respectively. Positions of sun, Earth, moon, and stars are schematically drawn in a view from the north celestial pole. The rotation of the Earth, revolution of the moon around the Earth, and revolution of the Earth together with the moon around the sun are counterclockwise and indicated by arrows. The innermost circle indicates the location of the sun in each of the twelve months of a year, expressed by twelve *chi* (支). Winter and summer solstices and vernal and autumnal equinoxes (in the earlier heaven) are shown in parentheses. This illustration indicates the positions of sun, moon, and Earth on the first day *kye mi* (癸未) of the first month *myo* (卯), New Year's Day of every year (in the later heaven).

There seem to be some suggestions of astronomical or physical changes in the Earth, the solar system, and the universe during a possible transitional critical period from the earlier heaven to the later heaven; however, no discrete or concrete changes are presented by Kim Il Bu in his book the *Jeong Yeok* (正易).

## The *Jeong Yeok*, the *Right Changes* of 360 Days of a Year

In the new age, one month has exactly thirty days in each of the twelve months of the year. There will be exactly 360 days in each year, without leap years. There will be mild weather, like spring and autumn, without severely hot summer and severely cold winter.

The above prediction may suggest that Earth's axis stands vertical to the plane of the ecliptic with a vanishing of the 23.5 degree tilt of the Earth's axis and the celestial equator (the "Red Road") and the celestial ecliptic (the "Yellow Road") united, and that there would be no seasons (H. A. Rey, *The Stars* [58]). A twenty-four *chyul* calendar in which each month is divided into two *chyul* (節) is appended to the *Jeong Yeok*. Kim Hang claimed that the *Jeong Yeok*, the *Right Changes,* is the original calendar and will be the ten thousandth generation's calendar in the coming age. Barbara Clow wrote in her book *The Mayan Code* [25] that the ancient Egyptians and Veda used a 360-day-year calendar five thousand years ago. To my knowledge, however, there seem to be no articles in the literature besides *The Mayan Code* that describe a year consisting of 360 days except the appendix of the *I Ching* (The Great Treatise, Part I, Chapter IX; Jeong Ho Yi [43]; James Legge [48]; Richard Willhelm [71]), in which Confucius suggested that a year of the coming new age would contain 360 days!

Kim Hang clearly indicated that his Il Bu's one year of the *Jeong Yeok* exactly coincides with Confucius's one year of 360 days. It seems to me that the new age will bring the Kingdom of God on Earth, and that the universe, the solar system, sun, Earth, and moon will probably, in their correct movements, generating an originally God-planned correct movement of the revolution of Earth around the sun in exactly 360 days.

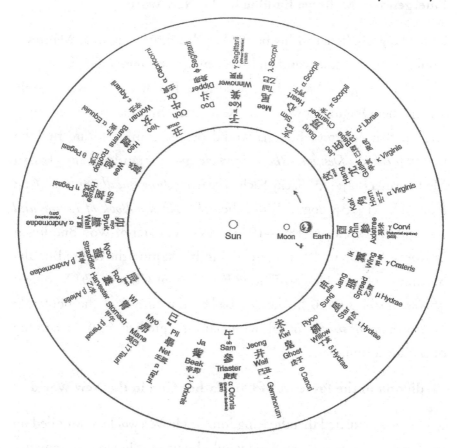

**Figure 1.** Star chart of the Twenty-Eight Lodges (宿, *Soo),* with corresponding Western reference stars. The middle and outer rings show the Twenty-Eight Lodges and corresponding Western reference stars, respectively. The rotation of the Earth, the revolution of the moon around the Earth, and the revolution of the Earth together with the

moon around the sun are counterclockwise and indicated by arrows. The inner ring indicates the location of the sun in each of twelve months of a year, expressed by twelve *chi* (支, branches). Winter and summer solstices and vernal and autumnal equinoxes (in the earlier heaven) are shown in parentheses (see text).

## Emergence of Maitreya Buddha in the New World

Kim Hang predicted in his book that the future Buddha, Maitreya, would be in the new world and the new age of *Yong-Hwa* (龍 華 歲 月), the "Dragon-Flower Era." Maitreya Buddha will teach people under the Dragon-Flower Tree. Gautama Buddha predicted in a sermon that Maitreya Buddha would be the coming future Buddha (*Anagatavamsa Desana: The Chronicle-to-Be,* translated by Udaya Meddegama [52]; [73]; Jacky Sach, *The Everything Buddhism Book* [61]; Jeong Ho Yi [73]; Sogyal Rinpoche, *The Tibetan Book of Living and Dying* [59]). So'taesan (1891–1943) was the master of Won Buddhism in Korea. He foretold to his disciples in his sermon the future Buddha Maitreya and the Dragon-Flower Era (Bongil Chung, *The Scriptures of Won Buddhism* [16]). Alice A. Bailey, the author of the book *The Reappearance of the Christ* [6], wrote about a prediction of the coming of Maitreya Buddha.

## Prediction of the Presence of Our Father God in the New World

Kim Hang predicted that the Kingdom of Heaven would be founded on the Earth and our Supreme God would be present in glorious radiance on Earth as in heaven.

The Creator God is expressed as the *Moogeuk* (无 極, Wu Chi), the Non-Ultimate, and is represented by the number ten in the *Jeong Yeok*. Action, or the process of activity of the *Moogeuk* in its beginning is expressed by the *Taegeuk* (太 極, T'ai Chi), the Great Ultimate and represented by the number one. The number five, halfway between ten and one, represents the *Hwanggeuk* (皇 極, Hwang Chi), the Ultimate Emperor that expresses man, sage, or son of God. All the other things of the universe are represented by the other numbers, two through nine. The real meaning of this numerology is unknowable to ordinary people.

It may be inferred that the *Taegeuk* (太 極), the Great Ultimate, might be the ultimate essence of quanta, the root of energy and consciousness enfolded in quanta. The *Taegeuk* seems to be "Word" (the logos-principle, 理, and possibly the "information" of David Bohm) that is action (用) of the *Moogeuk* and has creative energy (氣). The universe is the manifestation of God's Word.

In the *Jeong Yeok* it is said that in the macrocosm there are three *weon* (元), origins: the *Moogeuk*, the Non-Ultimate; the *Hwanggeuk*, the Ultimate Emperor; and the *Taegeuk*, the Great Ultimate. It seems to me inferable that in the microcosm—that is, in a human being—there are three selves: the super self, the inner self, and the physical self, as described in the Chapters 5 to 7, and they seem to most likely correspond to the *Moogeuk*, the *Hwanggeuk*, and the *Taegeuk*, respectively. The physical self and body originated from and are composed of the *Taegeuk* (太 極), the Great Ultimate, and developed with the principles of yin and yang as female and male and the five *heng* (行), elements. The inner self is created by and from the *Moogeuk* (无極), the Non-Ultimate, becoming the *Hwanggeuk* (皇極), the Ultimate Emperor. The super self would be part of the *Moogeuk*. Man is believed to represent a union of the *Moogeuk*, the *Hwanggeuk*, and the *Taegeuk*.

## The New Civilization of the New World

The light of God will gloriously illuminate heaven and earth. The sun and moon will brightly shine. A glossy, beautiful world will be born. The Yellow River will become clean once more. Correct human relations, propriety (called 禮, *ye*), and beautiful music (樂) will prevail in human society.

The *I Ching* and the *Jeong Yeok* predict that the ending and the recommencing of all the things of the world will be accomplished in the nation *Kan* (艮) of the east, which is expressed by the Eight *Kan* (a symbol of a mountain) in the diagram of the *Jeong Yeok* Eight Trigrams.

*Kan* (艮) is situated in northeast in the *Mun Wang* (文 王) Eight Trigrams, suggesting that all things of human history of the earlier heaven that began in *Jin* (震) in the east will come to an end in the Nation *Kan* (艮). After metal and fire change their positions in the *Lak Seo* (洛 書) that is basis of the *Mun Wang* (文 王) Eight Trigrams, moving to the original positions in the *Ha Do* (河 圖) that is the basis of the *Jeong Yeok* (正 易) Eight Trigrams, *Kan* (艮) moves to its correct position in the east and will start all things of the later heaven.

Confucius said in the Discussion of the Trigrams (設 卦 傳), describing the future *Jeong Yeok* (正 易) Eight Trigrams, "Therefore, water and fire complement each other, thunder and wind do not interfere with each other, and the forces of mountain and lake are united in their action. Thus only are change and transformation possible, and thus only can all things come to perfection" (Richard Willhelm, *The I Ching or Book of Changes* [71], Jeong Ho Yi [72], [74]).

The Nation *Kan* (艮) will unite with the Nation *Tae* (兌) of the West, expressed by the "Three Tae" (a symbol of a lake), and interchange their influences; that is, the spiritual culture of the East and the scientific civilization of the West will harmoniously join; thereafter, they will be able to change and transform human society and nations, and to give completion to all things in humanity, making enormous contributions to the coming of the new age and the new world. It is believed by students of the Kim Hang's philosophy that the *Kan* (艮) in the *Jeong Yeok* (正易) Eight Trigrams indicates an Eastern nation, being very suggestive of Korea as a leading country of the East, and that the *Tae* (兌) indicates a Western nation, being very suggestive of America as a main country of the West. Then the East and the West will unite and become one world under the heavens. The *Jeong Yeok* (正易) calendar will be used internationally, replacing lunar and solar calendars. The Kingdom of God will be established on the Earth. The Father, the Supreme God, will be present on Earth as in heaven. Humanity will become one family under heaven, enjoying peace, justice, sharing, and happiness with brotherhood and sisterhood. Goodness will be boundless in humanity. The civilization of the new world is unimaginable.

Christianity (represented by Jesus Christ), Confucianism (represented by Confucius and Kim Hang) seem to teach the same thing about the new age and the foundation of the Kingdom of God on Earth that is the plan of God and the will of God, giving humanity boundless hope.

I humbly and respectfully write the above sacred stories, seeking a true new world and praying to God for his grace and love.

January 5, 2008

**The Ha Do**                                      河　圖

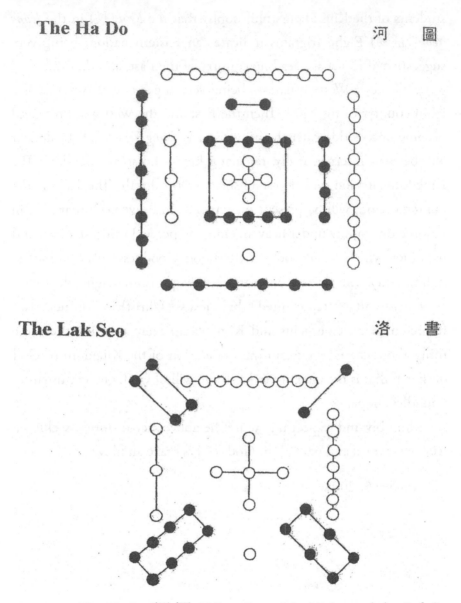

**The Lak Seo**                                    洛　書

**Figure 2.** The *Ha Do* (河 圖, Yellow River Map) Map and the *Lak Seo* (洛 書, the Writing from the River Lo) Writing. The upper diagram is the Ha Do Map, and the lower is the Lak Seo Writing (see text).

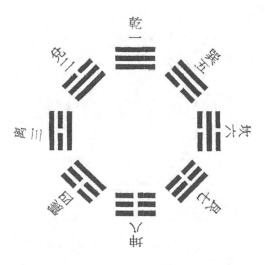

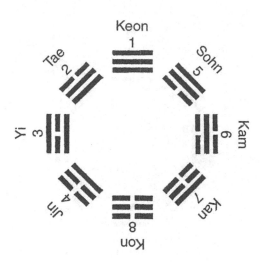

**Figure 3.** Diagram of the *Bok Hui* (伏 羲, Fu Hsi) Eight Trigrams. The upper diagram is the original diagram, and the lower is a translated one (see text).

文王八卦圖

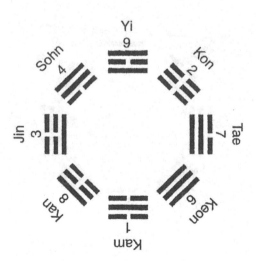

**Figure 4.** Diagram of the *Mun Wang* (文王, King Wen) Eight Trigrams. The upper diagram is the original diagram, and the lower is a translated one (see text).

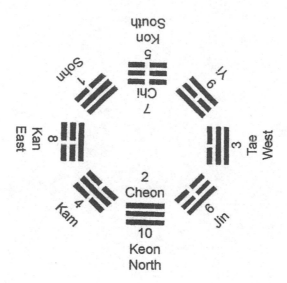

**Figure 5.** Diagram of the *Jeong Yeok* (正 易) Eight Trigrams. The upper diagram is the original diagram, and the lower is a translated one (see text).

# Epilogue

The new quantum theories in modern physics proposed by David Bohm, a great physicist, are based on particle-like and wave-like dual properties of elementary particles such as electrons and photons, proven by Nobel laureate Richard Feynman, and their timeless and non-local behavior and movements in which Einstein's relativity theory and the speed limit of light do not apply.

Richard Feynman said, "Nobody understands quantum mechanics." David Bohm said, "The law of flowing movement of wholeness, the totality that is the deeper foundation of quanta is unknown (probably unknowable)." It seems to me that these statements mean that no scientists understand wholeness and its law of holographic, flowing movement without borders, the world beyond the knowable quantum realm at the present time, the twenty-first century.

The laws described in the *Jeong Yeok* (正易) seem to me to probably represent the super-science of a new, higher order, seemingly the law of wholeness that David Bohm referred to. The terms used in the *Jeong Yeok* seem to be a priori and difficult for ordinary people to comprehend. *Yeok* (易) is so comprehensive and variable and indeed indefinable. It means "change"; a calendar; process of change; movement of the sun, moon, and Earth; law of creation; and probably plan of God. As Confucius said in his commentaries on the *I Ching* (Appendix III, Section I, Chapter IX), "The Master said: Whoever knows the Tao (道), the way of change and transformation, knows the action of the gods." Words, terms, and statements in the *Jeong Yeok* appear to suggest "information," as used by David Bohm. Those words, letters, and statements like the "information" of Bohm seem to be inherently powerful, persistent, creative, existing, evolving, and most likely representative of the law of wholeness and the foundation of the universe.

I would like to suggest that readers of this book have an open mind or an empty mind in order to see or imagine the world of wholeness that probably reflects its shadow in our physical world of reality. Though I have studied the *Jeong Yeok* for my whole life, the real meaning of the *Jeong Yeok* is quite unknowable to me. At least we ordinary people may possibly interpret and vaguely understand by applying our modern science and physics to the statements described in the *Jeong Yeok,* though they are beyond our comprehension, as I mentioned in chapters 11 and 12.

It seems to me, to my knowledge, that there is no translation in English of the original *Jeong Yeok* published in Korea, although it was partly introduced to the Western world by Jung Young Lee

I would like to recommend that readers read Lee's book *The Theory of Change* and his article "The Origin and Significance of the Chongyok or Book of Correct Change" in order to study the *Jeong Yeok* and the *I Ching.*

I would like to take full responsibility for any errors that I may have made in my writings and commentaries about the *Jeong Yeok* (正易). I humbly pray that the errors will be corrected in the future.

# REFERENCES

1. Adam. *The Path of the Dream Healer.* Dutton, New York, 2006 (xix, 66).

2. Applegate, George. *The Complete Book of Dowsing.* Element, Rockport, Massachusetts, 1997 (xiii, xvii, 37–54, 156, 196–7).

3. Armstrong, Karen. *Islam.* The Modern Library, New York, 2002 (189).

4. Aspect, Alain, J. Dalibard, and G. Roger. "Experimental test of Bell's inequalities using time-varying analyzer." *Physical Review Letters* 49 (1982): 1804–7.

5. Bache, Christopher M. *Lifecycles.* Paragon House, New York, 1994 (86, 110).

6. Bailey, Alice A. *The Reappearance of the Christ.* Lucis Publishing Co., New York, 2006.

7. ———. *The Consciousness of the Atom.* Lucis Publishing Co., New Lucis Publishing Co., New York, 1981 (83).

8. Beyer, Rick. *The Greatest War Stories Never Told.* HarperCollins, New York, 2005 (30).

9. Blasiola, George C. II. *Koi.* Baron's Educatonal Series, Inc., Hauppauge, New York, 1995 (80, 101).

10. Bohm, David. *Wholeness and the Implicate Order.* Routledge, New York, 2006.

11. Braunwald, Eugene, Anthony S. Fauci, Dennis L. Kasper, Stephen L. Hauser, Dan L. Longo, J. Larry Jameson, ed. *Harrison's Principles of Internal Medicine,* 15th Ed. McGraw-Hill, New York, 2001 (1069).

12. Buhlman, William. *Adventures Beyond the Body.* HarperSanFrancisco, New York, 1996 (37–68, 72).

13. Byrd, Randolph V. "Positive therapeutic effects of intercessory prayer in coronary care population." *Southern Medical Journal* 81 (1988):826–9.

14. Capra, Fritjof. *The Tao of Physics*. Shambhala Publications, Boston, 1999 (77, 88, 117, 225, 319).

15. Cerminara, Gina. *Many Mansions: The Edgar Cayce Story on Reincarnation*. Signet Books, New York, 1999 (276).

16. Chung, Bongkil. *The Scriptures of Won Buddhism*. University of Hawaii Press, Honolulu, 2005 (12, 342).

17. Chung, Sung J. "Studies of positive radial acceleration on mice." *Journal of Applied Physiology* 14 (1959) 52–4.

18. ———. "Studies on a mathematical relationship between stress and response in biological phenomena." *The Republic of Korea Journal of the National Academy of Sciences* 2 (1960) 115–62.

19. ———. "Computer-assisted predictive mathematical relationship among Metrazol and time and mortality in mice." *Computer Methods and Programs in Biomedicine* 22 (1986) 275–84.

20. ———. "Formula predicting the percentage of serum cholesterol levels by age in adults." *Archives of Pathology and Laboratory Medicine* 114 (1990) 869–75.

21. ———. "Formula expressing life expectancy, survival probability and death rate in life tables at various ages in US adults." *International Journal of Biomedical Computing* 39 (1995) 209–17.

22. ———. "Computer-assisted predictive formulas expressing survival probability and life expectancy in U.S. adults, men and women, 2001." *Computer Methods and Programs in Biomedicine* 86 (2007) 197–209.

23. Clow, Barbara Hand. *The Mayan Code*. Bear & Company, Rochester, Vermont, 2007 (44).

24. Cull, Christopher. *Astronomy and Mathematics in Ancient China*: *Zhou bi sun jing*. Cambridge University Press, Cambridge, UK, 1996 (17–8).

25. Dalai Lama, His Holiness the. *The Universe in a Single Atom*. Morgan Road Books, New York, 2005 (35, 38).

26. ———. "How To See Yourself As You Really Are." Atria Books, New York, 2006 (160, 185).

27. Edward, John. *One Last Time*. Berkley, Books, New York, 1999 (25, 35, 135, 156, 168).

28. ———. *Crossing Over*. Princess Books, New York, 2001 (153–5, 356).

29. Emoto, Masaru. *The Secret Life of Water*. Atria Books, New York, 2005 (16, 28, 48, 71–102).

30. Fuller, John G. *Arigo: Surgeon of the Rusty Knife*. Pocket Books, New York, 1975 (5, 56, 120, 193, 206).

31. Geller, Uri. *Mind Medicine*. Element Books, Boston, 1999.

32. Genz, Henning. *Nothingness: The Science of Empty Space*. Basic Books, New York, 1999 (235).

33. Gerber, Richard. *Vibrational Medicine*. Bear & Company, Rochester, Vermont, 2001.

34. Grey, Margot. *Return from Death*. Arkana, London, 1985 (101).

35. Gribbin, John. *Quantum Physics*. DK Publishing, New York, 2002 (60).

36. Gruenberg, Leif, A. *Defining Moments: The Korean War*. Omnigraphics, Detroit, Michigan, 1959 (xx, xxii, 29–38, 51–63, 65–8, 110–2).

37. Harris, William S., Manohar Gowda, and Jerry W. Kolby, et al., "A randomized control trial of the effetcs of remote intercessory prayer on outcomes in patients admitted to the coronary care unit." *Archives of Internal Medicine* 159 (1999) 2273–8.

38. Hastings, C., Jr. *Approximation for Digital Computer.* Princeton University Press, Princeton, New Jersey, 1955 (185).

39. Hastings, Max. *The Korean War.* Simon & Schuster, New York, 1987 (52, 99).

40. Hawkins, David R. *Power vs. Force: The Hidden Determinants of Human Behavior.* Hay House, Carlsbad, California, 2002 (291).

41. Hawking, Stephen. *A Brief History of Time: The Universe in a Nutshell.* Bantam Books, New York, 1996, 2001.

42. Kaku, Michio. *Physics of the Impossible.* Anchor Books, New York, 2008.

43. Kim, Hang. 정역 正易, *Jeong Yeok.* The original Chinese text with the text translated in Korean by Jeong Ho Yi. Asian Culture Press, Seoul, Korea, 1990 (60, 61, 76, 121).

44. Lao Tzu. *The Tao Te Ching.* Translated by Man-Ho Kwok, Martin Palmer, and Jay Rammy. Element Books, Rockport, Massachusetts, 1993 (98).

45. Laszlo, Ervin. *Science and the Akashic Field.* Inner Traditions, Rochester, Vermont, 2007 (7, 31).

46. Lee, Jung Young. *The Theory of Change.* Orbis Books, New York, 1979.

47. ———. "The origin and significance of the Chongyok or Book of Changes," *Journal of Chinese Philosophy* 9 (1982) 211–41.

48. Legge, James (translated). *The I Ching.* Dover Publications, New York, 1963 (1, 366, 427).

49. Lowenstein, Tom. *Buddhist Inspirations.* Duncan Bairs Publishers, London, 2005 (65).

50. Maitrya, Ananda (translated). *The Dhammapada.* Forward by Thich Nhat Hanh. Parallax Press, Berkley, California, 1995.

51. Mehta, S. C. and H. C. Joshi. "Model-based point estimates of survival/death rates: an input for radiation risk evaluation in Indian context." *Indian Journal of Nuclear Medicine* 19 (2004) 16–8.

52. Meddegama, Udaya (translated). *Anagatavamsa Desana: The Chronicle-To-Be.* Edited with an introduction, glossary, and notes by John Clifford Holt. Motilal Banarsidass Publishers, Delhi, India, 1993.

53. Müller, Max and V. Fausboll. *Dhammapadapali and Suttanipata.* Bharatyya Vidya Prakaham, Dehli, 2004.

54. Nichol, Lee. *The Essential David Bohm.* Routledge, New York, 2006.

55. O'Loughlin, Andrew. *Famous Precognitive and Problem-Solving Dreams and Others.* Carlton Press, New York, 1990.

56. Playfair, Guy Lyon. *Twin Telepathy.* Vega, London, 2002 (38, 92, 94, 121, 147).

57. Polanyi, Karl. *The Great Transformation.* Beacon Press, Boston, 2001.

58. Rey, H. A. *The Stars.* Houghton Mifflin Company, Boston, Massachusetts, 1980 (118, 134).

59. Rinpoche, Sogyal. *The Tibetan Book of Living and Dying.* HarperSanFrancisco, New York, 1993 (270).

60. Ross, Frank, Jr. *Oracles, Bones, Stones and Wheelbarrows: Ancient Chinese Science and Technology.* Houghton Mifflin Company, Boston, Massachusetts, 1982 (14).

61. Sach, Jacky. *The Everything Buddhism Book.* Adams Media Corporation, Avon, Massachusetts, 2003 (27, 122, 171).

62. Sardar, Ziauddin. *What Do Muslims Believe? The Roots and Realities of Modern Islam.* Walker Publishing Co., New York, 2007 (61, 75, 113, 115).

63. Schwartz, Gary E. *The Afterlife Experiments.* Pocket Books, New York, 2002 (124, 291–319).

64. Schwartz, Gary E., Linda G. S. Russek, Lonnie A. Nelson, and Christopher Barentsen. "Accuracy and replicability of anomalous after-death communication across highly skilled mediums." *Journal of the Society for Psychical Research* 65 (2001) 1–25.

65. Steiger, Brad. *One with the Light*. Signet Books, New York, 1994 (11, 31, 145).

66. Talbot, Michael. *The Holographic Universe*. HarperPerennial, New York, 1992 (46).

67. Targ, Russell and Jane Katra. *Miracles of Mind*. New World Library, Nevato, California, 1999 (6, 107–9).

68. Ullman, Montague, Stanley Krippner, and Alan Vaughan. *Dream Telepathy*. Hampton Roads Publishing Co., Charlottesville, Virginia, 2002.

69. Watson, Andrew. "Quantum Spookiness Wins, Einstein Loses in Photon Test," *Science* 277 (1997) 481.

70. Wech, Cindi Goodenough. *The Dream Seer*. Virtualbookworm. com Publishing Inc., College Station, Texas, 2003 (124).

71. Wilhelm, Richard. *The I Ching or Book of Changes*. Translated by Cary F. Baynes. Rutledge & Kegan Paul, London, 1967 (272, 309, 311).

72. Yi, Jeong Ho. *Jeong Yeok Yeongoo* (text in Korean). Kookjae University Press, Seoul, Korea, 1996 (203, 215, 224).

73. ———. *The I Ching Jeongi* (text in Korean). Asian Culture Press , Seoul, Korea, 1980, (71, 175)

74. ———. *The Third Yeok Hak* (text in Korean). Asian Culture Press, Seoul, Korea, 1992 (62, 150).

75. Yogananda, Pramahansa. *Spiritual Diary*. Self-Realization Fellowship, Los Angeles, California, 1996 (January 31, February 10, December 30).

Printed in the United States
by Baker & Taylor Publisher Services